Praise for *The Retail Doctor's*® *Guide to Growing Your Business*

"DON'T BUY THIS BOOK IF YOU ARE A COMPETITOR OF MINE!—but otherwise Bob Phibbs has great advice that that will enable you to make more money and have a successful business."

—Tom Sullivan, Chairman/Founder, Lumber Liquidators

"There's no denying that retailers have taken a beating lately. But the smart ones find a way to stop the bleeding and start looking ahead for new opportunities. With his plainspoken style and real-world anecdotes, Bob Phibbs gets back to basics and provides a helpful guide for entrepreneurs determined to survive the current downturn—and position themselves for the next big upswing."

—Rod Kurtz, Senior Editor, *Inc.* magazine

"Everyone knows that it is important to gain sales, but most do not know what that really takes or how to do it. This book will lead you on a journey that describes, analyzes, and provides real world examples how to really affect change with your business. If you will follow the treatment given, you'll be rewarded with the most important measures of a business's success— profits, not just sales."

—Georgette Mosbacher, President and CEO, Borghese Cosmetics

"Bob Phibbs presents more useful information in his typically direct and thought-provoking style that challenges you to really assess the performance of your business, your employees, and most importantly yourself. We often talk about personality types in leadership training and development, but it is not typically thought about in relation to the customer. Bob shows how these personality types play a role for you, your employees, and your customer, and how it can be most useful in looking for new approaches."

—Kurt Rachdorf, Retail Operations Senior Manager, LEGO

"Phibbs' no-nonsense approach to understanding your business and how to improve it is direct and refreshing. The concept of being objective and taking responsibility for your business can quickly make all the difference between success and failure, and Bob brings that to the table right from the start of this book. Great inspiration for any business owner!"

—Jeff Janke, Vice President, Retail Alliance Programs,
Hunter Douglas Window Fashions

"Bob blends his extensive retail experience and his direct style to tell it like it is. As retailers, we may not always like what he says, but it's hard to argue with the basics of running a successful business. In a market influenced by almost endless competition for the consumer's dollar, retailers need to continually ask themselves tough questions about what TRULY differentiates their offering.

Bob effectively reminds us of this hard reality. Bob's analytical approach allows us to better understand the filter through which we see our businesses. Only by adjusting our focus are we able to evaluate the true state of affairs.

—Alistair Linton, Director of Retail Development, Benjamin Moore Paints

"During my 30 years in the small business arena, Bob stands out as a 'pro's pro' in retail marketing. If you're determined to accelerate your growth, his street-smart book is a must. Buy it, read it, do it!"

—Steve Olson, Publisher, Franchise Update Media Group

"Phibbs' new book addresses everything necessary to take the pulse of your retail operation so you can find the cure. Whether it's managing staff, merchandising, or producing real sales, it prescribes a hands-on, real world, step-by-step approach to managing your business. Good news! The Doctor is in the house."

—Joseph Dagley, Yamaha Motor University

"Bob Phibbs has been my go-to retail expert for many years and his book shows why: he draws from a deep well of knowledge, presenting his advice in practical, easy-to-digest fashion. By explaining how entrepreneurs can evaluate themselves and their customers, Phibbs tailors this book to specific individual types that retailers will be quick to recognize. This is not a shallow primer, but a comprehensive prescription from The Retail Doctor®."

—Karen E. Klein, Small Business Columnist,
BusinessWeek.com and the *Los Angeles Times*

"Nothing in business is guaranteed. However, *The Retail Doctor's® Guide to Growing your Business* is guaranteed to help you gain insight into the do's and don'ts of successful retailing. Consider this book your survival manual to compete in the challenging world of retail."

—Dean F. Shulman Sr., Vice President, Brother International

"If you want to grow your business, the book in your hand right now is the place to start. Bob Phibbs is one of the top retail experts in the country; he's not called The Retail Doctor® for nothing. This step-by-step guide will show you—using real life examples and savvy strategies—just how to get from here to where you want to be. My prescription for small business success is to read *The Retail Doctor's® Guide to Growing Your Business.*"

—Steven D. Strauss, *USA Today* Small Business Columnist
and author of *The Small Business Bible.*

"Bob's approach is no-nonsense, and his back-to-basics philosophy is something a lot of retailers need to hear right now. I would advise keeping a highlighter handy."

—James Bickers, Senior Editor, RetailCustomerExperience.com

THE
RETAIL
DOCTOR'S®

GUIDE TO

GROWING YOUR
BUSINESS

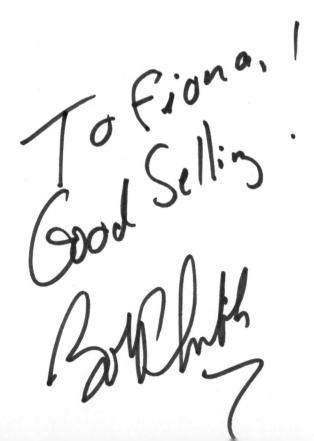

To Fiona,!

Good Selling.

Bob Phibbs

THE
RETAIL DOCTOR'S®

GUIDE TO
GROWING YOUR BUSINESS

A **STEP-BY-STEP** APPROACH TO QUICKLY **DIAGNOSE, TREAT,** AND **CURE**

BOB PHIBBS

WILEY

John Wiley & Sons, Inc.

Published by John Wiley & Sons, Inc., Hoboken, New Jersey
Published simultaneously in Canada

The Retail Doctor is a registered trademark® of Bob Phibbs.

For general information on our other products and services or for technical support, please contact our Customer Care Department within the United States at (800) 762-2974, outside the United States at (317) 572-3993 or fax (317) 572-4002.

Wiley also publishes its books in a variety of electronic formats. Some content that appears in print may not be available in electronic books. For more information about Wiley products, visit our web site at www.wiley.com.

Library of Congress Cataloging-in-Publication Data:

Phibbs, Bob.
  The retail doctor's guide to growing your business : a step-by-step approach to quickly diagnose, treat, and cure / by Bob Phibbs.
    p. cm.
  ISBN 978-0-470-58717-1 (pbk.)
  e-ISBNs 978-0-470-58717-1, 978-0-470-63648-0, 978-0-470-63647-3
  1. Retail trade–Management. 2. Small business–Growth. 3. Small business–Management. I. Title.
  HF5429.P54 2010
  658.8'7–dc22

                                                                                    2010000759

Printed in the United States of America

10 9 8 7 6 5 4 3

Contents

Acknowledgments

Jessica Faust, my agent who saw that now was the right time for this book. Lauren Lynch, who believed in my positive message of change, her production editor Kate Lindsay, and the team at John Wiley & Sons, Inc., who put up with my, "just one more thing." Ruth Rawlings and Nancy Himel, who provided early feedback, especially in the organization of sections. Barry Busler, who made all the quizzes on the web site functional. All the reviewers who took their time to read and critique the manuscript including, James Bickers, Joseph Dagley, Jeff Janke, Karen Klein, Rod Kurtz, Alistair Linton, Georgette Mosbacher, Steve Olson, Kurt Rachdorf, Dean Shulman, Steven Strauss, and Tom Sullivan. To my writing mentors, Terrie Silverman and Jack Grapes in Los Angeles, who kept me focused on keeping my voice in print. To business mentors who I have learned from over the years including Tom Antion, Patricia Fripp, Peter Glen, Tom Hopkins, John McKeon, and Zig Ziglar.

The thousands of employees, managers, and owners I have had the privilege to work with and learn from on the way to higher sales.

Introduction

What's Ailing You?

It was famed football coach Vince Lombardi who said, "Adversity doesn't build character. It reveals character." We have just come through one of the most wrenching periods for business in 50 years. Assumptions about consumer spending, good locations, and products that sell have been upended. Marketing tools you've used for years have suddenly stopped working. Things to which you may have not paid attention are now demanding that you do. And so you've purchased this book to help you learn how to make your business more profitable. Congratulations.

How do you know when you're sick and need a doctor's help? If you're like most of us, when you start having headaches, running a fever, get nauseous, or just feeling lousy, you probably think about calling the doctor. When it's a business struggling with symptoms like cash flow, employee turnover, and low sales, thousands have looked to me as the Retail Doctor® to help them.

You've come here looking for answers or a silver bullet that will make all your dreams come true. It's human nature to want the easy way out: the *one thing* that will alter your world and point to happiness. But it's a series of small actions that makes the difference.

In that respect, nothing has changed since retailers first began. What drove me to write this book now is that I haven't seen a straightforward approach to building a business in a concise easy-to-use style.

So much of the recent news is filled with tales of cutting costs and discounting—a fast track to the going-out-of-business sale. You can't use external circumstances like the economy as an excuse to not change.

You have to take responsibility for the things you can control: that which takes place inside your four walls. The recession that started in 2006 affected all businesses: No one was granted an advantage, a hindrance, or a get-out-of-jail-free card. Even in a recession, companies rose and fell based on their attitude toward the challenge of gaining new customers, holding onto existing ones, and giving both a compelling reason to return.

But how do you do it? The path to your success is to find the leverage to change the way you do business and resist any fear of change. *The Retail Doctor's*® *Guide to Growing Your Business* will help you accomplish this. It will jolt you out of your complacency, give you new tools to look at your challenges, and send you on your way with renewed confidence that you are able to change your situation.

No, the silver bullet is not a person, a product, a display, or new vendor—it's you. *You* are the one thing that can have maximum effectiveness. Disappointed with your store's performance? Sorry, it's up to you to improve it. Distressed about the fact that fewer customers are coming in? Sorry, it's up to you to find some new ones. Unhappy that you've got stockpiles of unsold merchandise? Sorry, it's up to you to figure out a way to get rid of it.

Store Performance Down? Well, What Are You Doing about It?

Have you fired Bitter Betty? We'll talk more about her later, and you'll learn about a sewing retailer in Virginia who I advised get rid of one particularly troublesome employee. Although she resisted for almost three years, when she finally did take my advice, she was astounded to find how many customers had avoided her store due to one bad employee.

Not making enough profits? Many owners price merchandise too low because they "know how much it really cost," but I'll show you why that "welfare pricing" structure could be killing you. Once you get your pricing right and your sales increasing, your percentages of labor and rent are reduced. In short, the rising tide of sales lifts all boats.

Unhappy with too much merchandise? Unsold merch is equivalent to your money sitting there. I'll show you new ways to analyze it, to take the money off the floor and put it into your bank account.

Distressed about a lack of customers? Well, what have you done lately to actively bring them back in? Do you have a mailing list, a web site, a blog, or a Facebook fan page? I'll cover all of that and why there has never been a better time to market your business. One Arizona toy store owner used e-mail blasts before and after every event to boost her sales by 20 percent. She embraced new marketing techniques that were financially effective and made it fun to connect with her customers—and you can, too.

My message to you is just like a doctor's would be if you were facing dire health consequences from inaction: "Change or die." There is no choice, no denial, and no silver bullet. The only thing standing in the way of you succeeding is you.

But who are you, anyway—a business owner, wife, son, teacher, employee? Those are roles. What I mean by this question is this: What traits, behaviors, and natural inclination do you use to look at the world? As I have helped thousands of businesses improve and grow, I've noticed that once I could get a thumbnail sketch of how the owner, manager, and employees were hard-wired, I could meet with greater success than if I expected everyone to be just like me.

That's why—before we get going on the financials—it is important to know a bit about your personality type, so I can help you understand some of the innate characteristics of your own and the other three main personalities. You can slice and dice personalities using a variety of personality profile methods—including the Meyers-Briggs, McQuaig Word Survey, and the DISC method. But for our purposes, there are basically four. Throughout the book, you'll discover how these four types play out when interacting with customers as well as training and rewarding employees.

Meet the Ruler of Your Business: The Brain or the Heart

Authors David Merrill and Roger Reid noted in their almost 30-year-old book, *Personal Styles and Effective Performance* (1981), that there

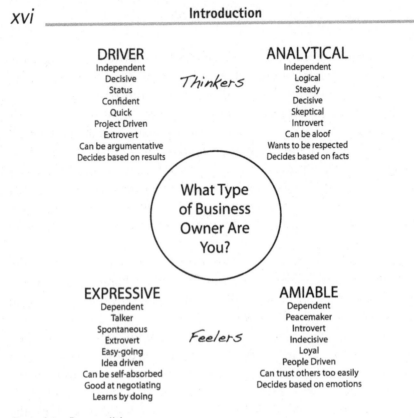

DRIVER
Independent
Decisive
Status
Confident
Quick
Project Driven
Extrovert
Can be argumentative
Decides based on results

Thinkers

ANALYTICAL
Independent
Logical
Steady
Decisive
Skeptical
Introvert
Can be aloof
Wants to be respected
Decides based on facts

What Type of Business Owner Are You?

EXPRESSIVE
Dependent
Talker
Spontaneous
Extrovert
Easy-going
Idea driven
Can be self-absorbed
Good at negotiating
Learns by doing

Feelers

AMIABLE
Dependent
Peacemaker
Introvert
Indecisive
Loyal
People Driven
Can trust others too easily
Decides based on emotions

FIGURE I.1   Personalities

are two main types of personality: those that are controlled by the brain (Thinkers) and those that are controlled by the heart (Feelers). Peter Urs Bender, author of *Leadership from Within* (1997), went on to say that each of those categories contains two subgroups of personalities for a total of four.

One of the Thinkers' distinct personality types is called Drivers. They represent about 6 percent of the population and are focused on results, and being the best, unique, and driven; think Donald Trump and his signature "You're fired" line. A Driver tends to be a showoff, brand conscious, and a bit of a braggart. Drivers need to be engaged and are frequently asking questions or jumping into discussions. Some people might describe Drivers as blunt or arrogant because they form opinions very easily and are quite sure of themselves. Drivers aren't afraid to take risks to get what they want. Think **ego** when you're talking about the Driver personality.

The second personality within the Thinkers is the Analytical. These people tend to ask a lot of "how" questions, and require things to make sense, be logical, or provide a good value. These types of personalities drive safe cars that come with a great guarantee, they may clip coupons, and they are no-frills. While the Driver could be the fighter pilot, the Analytical is the bomber pilot with the motto "steady as she goes." Picture the character Spock from *Star Trek* when thinking about the Analyticals, which represent about 32 percent of the population. Think *facts* when you're talking about the Analytical personality.

The other main group—the Feelers, who are ruled by their hearts—also has two personality subtypes. Representing only 9 percent of the population, the first group is called the Expressives. Think Jimmy Buffett of Margaritaville fame, Sam Malone from the TV show *Cheers*, or comedienne Kathy Griffin. These people want to know who is going to be at the party. They live life to the fullest, are not detail-oriented or likely to over think a response but like to show off. They are essentially the opposite of the Analytical personality. If they were dogs at the dog park, they'd be the Black Labradors running around with a bone for someone to throw for them. These are the people who are the spark plugs to life; think *fun* experiences.

The fourth of the personality types—the Amiables—is the heart and soul of our communities. Think Charlotte York from *Sex and the City* or Dorothy from *The Wizard of Oz*. The Amiable is the most likely personality type you will encounter. These are the peacemakers: teachers, nurses, caregivers, and volunteers. They want to serve the greater good and know about what others prefer. These people are all over social media sites like Facebook and Flickr. They do not make waves and are more comfortable making others happy and being liked than taking a stand. They are the opposite of the Driver and represent 53 percent of the population. Think *caring* when you picture the Amiable.

Take Your Exam

Before you go further, please take this quick online personality test at www.retaildoc.com/personality-quiz/.

When you identify your personality's strengths and weaknesses, you're able to listen and respond in the appropriate manner, to the other three personalities, not simply in the way that comes naturally to your personality.

Now that you have a sense of how you look at the world, consider the personalities of your employees and colleagues. In order to get the most from them, you'll want to speak in language they all understand. For example: I have learned that my weakness as a Driver is a get-to-the-point attitude that can distance me from others. Being aware of this allows me to find ways to make fun of that tendency and, at times, bite my tongue to make sure I don't shut down or scare off an Expressive or Amiable personality. It doesn't always work, but I know that is my Achilles heel.

How Your Personality Type Affects Your Business

Where you and your employees fall in the Thinkers and Feelers personality spectrum directly affects your company's profitability. For example: It's rare to find an Amiable as a manager, but not unusual to find one as a business owner. Because they approach the world with their hearts, they tend to hire other Amiables to make friends with them. That may stunt their business' results, however, because they give second, third, and fourth chances to erring employees whom Drivers or Analyticals would have fired. By their very nature, Amiables want to concentrate on what they are doing right rather than look for areas that need improvement and feel bad about themselves.

Drivers can be ineffective bosses in that they tend to focus solely on results, which can create a pressure cooker atmosphere if they aren't careful. "They stay until they cost me money" is a common Driver attitude toward new employees. While Expressives can be fun managers, you often end up with several half-finished projects while you learn all about their personal lives and what they did last night. They're great at coming up with ideas but not the best at following through. And Analyticals can be ineffective leaders because they don't offer much praise. Because their logical skills mask their humanity, it's expected by them that you showed up and made a great sale.

All four groups have their own challenges and insights, all of which are equally important. Throughout the book, you'll encounter each type of personality manifested by customers, colleagues, and salespeople. You'll see what each might bring to your store, how they tend to behave as managers, and what skills you need to develop to communicate effectively with the various types.

In addition, I find that when a particular business is not making as much money as the owner would like, it often stems from the owner's or manager's viewing the business through the eyes of the customer rather than the merchant. Analyticals and Drivers come naturally to calculating results like a merchant; Amiables and Expressives naturally empathize with others and view results like a customer. Do you make personal statements like the following?

- "I don't like it when a store like Macy's uses asterisks to note all those exclusions on a discount. I think it's a rip-off." That's thinking like a customer Feelers. Putting the whole store on sale often means that you sell out of your best items quickly and have less money to restock. Limiting discounts is thinking like a merchant.
- "I don't like it when employees glom all over you. I just want to help myself. If I need help, I'll ask. Until then, just leave me alone." That's thinking like every customer is like you Analyticals. Piles of merchandise can't do the heavy lifting of driving sales like a well-trained salesperson.
- "I don't like it when someone tries to sell me something. They only want to push what they have on me." Identifying yourself as an untrusting customer makes you feel like a fraud—and makes selling your merch that much harder for you.
- "I don't like seeing holiday merchandise until after Thanksgiving." A smart merchant realizes there are only so many days until a holiday, and if the big boys are doing it, there must be a reason.
- "I wouldn't pay that much for this item." Knowing how much something costs at wholesale somehow devalues its worth in your eyes and causes you to think like a customer. Therefore, you don't usually set the price high enough to make a profit.

Sympathizing with customers shows up in marketing and promotions with endless freebies, 2-for-1s, or discounts. I know of one local gift store that offered free gift-wrapping on Valentine's Day. It was the store's busiest day of the year—a day when people would have paid anything to have someone wrap their gifts—and the store gave it away. How on earth did the owner make that decision? He must have envisioned how great the customers would feel. Imagine a florist giving free same-day delivery on Mother's Day or a liquor store offering 25 percent off champagne on December 31? Wouldn't that be great, too? But the intent to "get" like a customer instead of "lose" like a merchant damages earnings; if you want to be profitable, you must focus on the bottom-line results.

The difference between Thinker and Feeler personalities manifests itself in the way you interact with employees. Instead of establishing a firm schedule he could complete in a half hour or so, a Feeler manager lets employees provide their availability week by week—and then tries to create a schedule around them. The result is hours and hours of wasted time and compromised store coverage. The problem is exacerbated when the Feeler doesn't penalize staff members for lateness, rudeness, or an inability to perform the job. Thinker personalities, however, tend to come up with a strict schedule based on demand, and then fill it based on their ability to sell the merch. That allows the managers much more time to train, monitor, and sell on the floor.

Much as thinking like a customer hinders the ability to make a profit, thinking like an employee cripples a manager's ability to perform his job as a merchant. They want to be "nice," "liked," "popular." I had a boss one time say, "You're only as good as your last sale." Brutal—and true. He was a Thinker, a Driver, a merchant.

By understanding the different mind-set of a merchant (typically a Thinker personality) versus a customer (usually a Feeler), anyone can adapt these traits to help make tough decisions. Simply ask yourself: "Am I thinking like a merchant looking to profitability or like a customer or employee looking for perks?" As my buddy—and well-known author—Randy Gage says, "Never let who you have been interfere with who you can become." Exactly.

You're going on a journey to explore your business, just like the process I use for business makeovers throughout the world. We'll examine your financials, then whip your four walls into shape by learning some secrets to merchandising, see how you select your employees, create a training program, and finally examine your marketing. It's going to be a profitable journey for you—so let's get going!

Chapter 1

Financials Are the Vital Signs to Measuring Your Success

In medicine, vital signs are basic measures of life and good health. Likewise, a business's financials are the vital signs that immediately determine whether it needs triage, treatment, or just TLC. Just as your temperature, blood pressure, and pulse are clear gauges of your *body's* health, your financials are the black-and-white indicators of your *company's* health. We begin with your company's numbers because they are the tools against which you measure your progress. If you can monitor something, you can affect it, because numbers don't lie.

Do you look at your financials every year? Every month? How about every week? If you are a Driver or Analytical—the Thinkers—the answer is probably yes. If you are an Expressive or Amiable you may already have thought of skipping ahead. *Please don't do that.* I had an owner tell me bluntly, "Bob, high volume covers a bunch of sins"—kind of like "the end justifies the means." The problem with that kind of thinking is that you can get high sales but with great damage to your profitability. You don't have to go any further than the big retailers like Saks, who heavily discount their premium goods to try to bring in customers, to see evidence of what I'm talking about.

We'll dig into the following key financial metrics for a business in this chapter:

◆ Profit and loss statement
◆ Pricing

- Sales by category
- Average sale
- Average number of items per transaction
- Number of transactions per customers
- Year-over-year to date

While this book is written from a retailer's point of view, most of these tools can be applied to any service, manufacturer, or other industry.

Leverage

Suppose you have a two-year-old daughter who depends on you for her well-being. If a doctor diagnoses you with lung cancer and warns that if you take another puff, you'll be dead, chances are good you would have sufficient leverage to quit smoking. Leverage gives you impetus for change. It's like an internal switch that flips once you've seen that the costs and consequences are greater if you stay the same. Leverage is not "I want to be the next Apple." Leverage is "if we don't increase our electronics business by 15 percent, I won't be able to afford payroll." Leverage is something you have to look for on your own.

Leverage requires that you see the consequences of *not* changing, feel the fear that this incites, and memorize it. Imagine your house foreclosed upon and your store vacant; try using *that* for leverage. Use whatever works to define failure for you. Every time you don't follow through with a change, remember this leverage clearly by seeing the alternative; that will stir you to action. Accessing your inner motivation to change means honestly appraising the results you want and using the proper leverage to follow through.

When I met Mike Sheldrake, the owner of Polly's Gourmet Coffee in Long Beach, California, in 1998, he had more debt than he had in sales. He had hoped something would change, but when it really came down to it, his back was against the wall. He looked at his profit and loss statement and saw the consequences of years of inaction.

Perhaps you're like Mike right now, paralyzed by your bottom line. Or maybe you have remained blissfully in the dark by only looking at gross sales numbers. But there is much more detail that could help you increase profits. The good news is that you can change your profit and loss statement by using the reporting tools you probably already have.

Now, you might say to me, "You don't understand, Bob, we had a great June . . . it was fabulous." But if we looked at the transaction count and found that you lost more than 100 customers, would you still consider it "fabulous"? And if you were to ask your manager why, he would probably answer, "I don't know."

Profit and Loss Statement

A profit and loss statement measures how much out of every dollar of sales a company actually keeps in earnings. (This is different from your product margin, which is the difference between the cost of the merchandise and your retail price.) A profit and loss statement shows your profit margin, which is net profit divided by sales. Here's something you must always keep in mind:

You have to be profitable.

Profits mean that customers are rewarding you for your efforts in excess of what it costs you to run the business. If you are not making a profit, the market is punishing you for poor management, meager product selection, inadequate location, or rotten employees. Losses mean someone is paying for your poor management: your bank, your other job, your savings, or your spouse. Profit margins must support what your business needs to pay the bills, debt load, the owner a salary, and a "draw" for your retirement fund.

Profit margin is displayed as a percentage. A 3 percent profit margin, for example, means the company has a net income of $0.03 for each dollar of sales. That is typically the profit for a successful small business, although each business model is different. The higher your profit margin is, the more control you have over your costs—which is a real competitive advantage.

If you have a competitor who's been around for 50 years and has no rent or financing costs, it may be able to sell cheaper than you. If you purchased your business with an adjustable home equity loan, that debt load may mean you need to charge more than your competitors. You might increase gross sales if you try to match your competitor's low prices, but you won't be earning enough money to garner a positive profit margin. You'll just continue to dig yourself deeper.

What *Exactly* Are You Losing?

I did a business makeover for a couple who owned a restaurant in southern California. After completing the evaluation, I had to give them the difficult news that they would make more money by closing than by trying to fix the myriad challenges. The husband seemed relieved as he'd been writing the checks to bail out the business, which employed their son as manager. The wife claimed to be okay with the fact that she'd been losing up to $11,000 each month for the past year and a half by saying that, "You have to lose money to make money." I was surprised and replied, "Okay, but this isn't a start-up; you've never made a profit or anything close." I continued, "Think of it this way. You are throwing away a brand-new Mercedes Benz—like the one you drive—every four months." *That* got her attention. There's losing money and then there's *losing money.*

How to Increase Your Profit Margins Based on Your Profit and Loss Statement

1. Increase prices. No one knows the price you pay but *you.* You can selectively raise the price of your most popular items to most effectively add to your bottom line; you don't have to increase prices across the board (see "Pricing" on page 8).
2. Narrow your focus. You can't be all things to all people. It's the difference between a restaurant with a menu of 200 mediocre items and one with 12 outstanding dishes. Consider how much profit you are making on your slower-moving items. Could that shelf space be devoted to quicker-moving, more profitable items? Yes!

3. Limit the discounting. Without a plan, you'll do anything to get money in. I know one toy store owner who, using Twitter, tells her followers they'll get 30 percent off if they come in that day. What she doesn't realize is how she is robbing herself of profits to pay bills.

4. Cut waste—or get more done with what you have. Are there jobs you're hiring others to do that you could possibly complete yourself? Do you really need to pay a window washer, for example?

5. Schedule to need. Do you have three people to open when two could do for the first couple hours? Likewise, add a staff member if you are slammed every Saturday, so you don't lose customers to a competitor.

6. No overtime. *Period.* Don't let hourly managers fill in for lower-cost hourly employees. Use salaried employees if something comes up.

7. Stop scheduling for convenience of employees. I don't care if Vivian does like working for eight hours. If all you need her for is four, then give her four.

8. Award extra hours based on merit. Grant employee requests for more hours based only on their average sale or number of units sold per customer, not simply on their request or need.

9. Make yourself hand out all paychecks, so you personally see how much each staff member makes.

10. Pay bonuses that are proportionate to the amount of profit the business brings in rather than total sales numbers. Otherwise, you could be rewarding an Expressive or Driver salesperson who discounts to make the sale robbing you of any profit.

11. Look for theft by matching inventory to sales. A restaurant franchise I know of audits for internal theft by simply matching how many cups it received to how many cold beverages the point-of-sale system said the restaurant sold in a certain time. The results can show lots of unpaid drinks, which affect profitability.

12. Clean out the stockroom. If it's in the back, it can't be sold. If it won't fit on the floor, why do you have it?

13. Cut vendors. When you buy more from fewer vendors, you'll often get a better deal on pricing, shipping, and dating. Ordering only a few items from a number of vendors requires more bookkeeping and tracking, and you often pay top dollar to try to meet each one's minimums. No one's items are *that* special.

14. Combine your orders with another dealer to get freight and larger order discounts. Just be sure to decide ahead of time which of you will do what, and pay before delivery to avoid problems.

15. Sell added value by bundling products and services; think Best Buy's Geek Squad. It promises it can "Fix any computer problem—anytime, anywhere." Of course, it leaves off: "For a price." People don't want the hassle of figuring things out or setting things up. Customers value their time and will pay for worthwhile services related to the products you carry. Selling added value is the way to a profitable future. For example, if you ran a store that sold items for parties you could offer to set up a customer's birthday party for an additional $100.

16. Fire unprofitable customers who need a lot of hand-holding, always beat you up on price, or constantly call you with some problem. If your company is large enough to evaluate this, ask your order desk or sales reps to provide their top 10 complainers and match them to the amount of profitable orders they generate. Even if they deliver large volume, if they don't pass, tell them that while you appreciate their business, the costs to manage the account outweigh the profitability and you therefore must implement a price increase.

The Lazy Owner's Way to Deal with POS Reports

When it comes to financial reports, many of us—with the exception of Analyticals—have little inclination to dwell on them. That's normal; if you enjoyed them you would have been an accountant, not a business owner. Most point-of-sale (POS) systems can run 300 to 400 reports to slice and dice the broadest trends to the smallest details of a single item. But who has time for all that?

Instead of trying to find the time to choose, create, and download the report you want, pay your service provider to have them automatically e-mailed to you every Monday morning. The right reports will give you the necessary information you need in real time, so you can correct any problems revealed before they affect your bottom line. Here's a list of eight reports—as well as information on what each one shows—that you'll want to review weekly:

1. **Average check**—the value of each customer that day.
2. **Number of transactions (also called customer count)**—the number of total sales tickets that were generated each day.
3. **Weekly sales by category**—your top and bottom five categories to help establish buying trends.
4. **Weekly sales by salesperson**—how much each employee contributes to sales per week.
5. **Year-over-year by week**—how you are doing compared to the same week of the previous year.
6. **Year-over-year to date**—a running total of your year-over-year sales to help you see the bigger trends in sales.
7. **Number of units per transaction**—how well your crew can upsell.
8. **Number of voids**—will alert you to a thief among your sales staff.

These reports allow you to go back to your manager and ask, "Did you notice our average number of units per transaction has gone down whenever Vicki is working? Why do you think that is?" He would have to have the answers if he still wants to be manager. Now imagine that you didn't have these reports, and you simply asked your manager, "Why are sales down?" He could just answer, "Because we're not getting the traffic we need." You would shake your head, have nowhere to go with the discussion, run more discounts, and/or dump more money into the business—without ever discovering the reasons *why* sales are down. This is especially true if you are a Feeler.

But looking over these reports on a regular basis lets you know that you have to retrain Vicki, move her to another shift, or help her realize that your company may not be the best place for her.

Pricing

Since many owners or managers have never taken a course on pricing or they "feel bad about charging too much," they tend to mark up less than necessary—what I call "welfare pricing." (In fact, I met a guy at a recent speech who sheepishly admitted he purchased an item for $20 and priced it at $25.) Your merchandise should be marked up "keystone" (that's double), plus enough extra to make the business profitable. Although many retailers feel that their margins are okay, the individual margins may not add up to be profitable for the business. Again, it's the merchant's duty to attend to the bottom line.

Simply put: an item has value if it is worth the price a customer is willing to pay. There's a deli truck in the park by my house that sells soda for 50 cents. I figure that the vendor can get a six-pack for a buck at the local big box. She might be telling herself she's getting three times the cost; but what would a customer pay for the convenience? A vending machine would charge at least $1. But the deli truck vendor gives you a cup and ice. Would that be worth $1.25? I think so. Sometimes you have to consider the value you provide to the customer and charge what you think the market can *afford*, not what *you* personally would pay.

Make sure when selecting promotional merchandise that you can feature a discounted price and still make a profit. Many retailers make the mistake of getting a one-time deal from a vendor, then passing the savings on to the customer and never taking the advantage of the difference themselves to boost profits. As a result, they put less cash in their bank accounts. If you can get a good deal on an item, price it to the expected market amount when it first arrives and see how it sells.

You also have to consider breakage, spoilage, and other items out of your control before you set a price. For example, a baker who has to bake a dozen rolls at a time might know he typically only sells seven of a certain roll every day. So he factors in that five might remain, and prices the seven to make the profit of all twelve. It's therefore a bonus if he sells out occasionally. If you own a nursery and lose 80 percent of the plants you start from seed, it might be cheaper in the long run to buy plants that have already been started instead of being wed to the notion of growing everything yourself. You'll use less labor and end up with more sellable merchandise and once you factor in all the costs, you may find it less expensive. Don't worry; there's no big customer police in the sky about to cry out, "Fraud!"

Contrary to what many owners believe, discounting is *not* the companion to pricing right. If you price too low to begin with, you often are selling the item for less than it cost to buy and ship to you when discounts are applied. It's easy for a Driver salesperson to say, "Oh sure, I'll take off an extra 15 percent," or, "I'll throw that in." That is not sales; that is cutting profits!

California-based clothing retailer Howard & Phil's Western Wear had a store manager that discounted in order to make sales—even though it was against stated company policy. Her store had the highest volume by a long shot. While it was common knowledge she was discounting, the owners didn't make her stop because they liked seeing the sales numbers. Unsurprisingly, the company eventually went bankrupt. Millions of dollars in sales mean *nothing* when there is no profit.

Any Accounting 101 student can tell you that the profit earned by the average business is only one to three cents on the dollar. This fact flies in the face of a common perception that small business owners are raking in the dough. Go ahead, ask your employees how much they think you keep out of every $100 sold—you'll be surprised.

When you're considering giving $10 off an item, realize that you have to sell at least $300 more just to earn back that $10 in profit. That's why you frequently find when you analyze discounts that—like a sugary cola drink—it gives you an added boost when you're tired. But like that sugary cola drink, the high is temporary and you eventually crash; discounting does nothing for your (or your company's) long-term health.

Your profit and loss statement is the snapshot of the overall health of your business: *the bottom line.* You'll need some more reports to compile a full diagnostic on where your business can improve.

Luckily, all of the information you need lies in the data you already have collected.

Sales by Category

As you're well aware, not every item contributes equally to your sales. Therefore, you look at the sales by category report to see how well your merchandise selections are supporting the business. Much like your skeleton supports your muscles and—well, everything else in your body—your profitability hangs on your assortment, pricing, discounts, and how well your products turn over. Reduce inventory in categories that aren't producing so that you can increase your bestsellers and limit new orders based on past sales. That's why you have to take an open-to-buy approach based on your sales by category if you want to increase profits.

Your Open-to-Buy

The temptation during a recession (like the recent one) is to cut everything 20 percent—from employee hours and total number of employees to advertising and office expenses. The trouble with this method is that you could end up being out of backups when employees call in sick or quit; off your customers' radar when they choose to buy your products from a competitor; or out of stock when customers came to you for it.

Selling your inventory is your only way to make money. Having a pretty store with piles of merch won't do the trick. That merch has to come and go on a regular basis or it will rot. Think of your inventory like you would fresh milk. Would you want to buy tens of gallons but end up with most of it spoiled? No, you manage fresh milk by how much you use. The same should be true of your merchandise. If you buy too much inventory, it, too, will go bad.

When you are buying merchandise, you're certainly *hopeful* that it will sell; but your orders have to be based on more than a hunch if you want to grow your business. Your stock levels must correspond with your most recent sales trends. For example, you can order 10 percent more merchandise if sales grew 10 percent in the previous two months. Monitoring your open-to-buy monthly makes you a smarter merchant because that is your money sitting on the sales floor.

In 2008, retail giant Nordstrom decided to shrink its year-end inventory per square foot 12 percent from the previous year, thereby reducing supplies in line with shrinking demand. That poised them for future growth with new merch rather than stockpiles of unsold goods like Macy's—a store that was trying to give the stuff away with 70 and 80 percent off.

Don't Hold on to Past Failures

If it didn't sell when it was new, don't think it suddenly will six months later when your employees are cold to it. It's best to identify as quickly as possible what is not performing, move it out, and bring in fresh merchandise. That allows you to get more of the right merch to grow profits.

While that *sounds* simple, you've likely had the experience of telling your manager, "We are going to get rid of X product because it's not selling," and had your manager reply, "We can't get rid of it, we sell tons of it!" Then you went to your POS reports and found you only sold a handful. That's because most employees remember most vividly their last sale or the last thing a customer requested that you didn't have. To get the big picture, you need to use your category sales report from your POS system to determine correct inventory levels. Otherwise, you might think an item being gone is reason enough to reorder. But missing stock could be due to demand *or* theft—customers taking it when no one is looking or employees lifting it as they take out the trash. You'll never know unless you look carefully at your category reports.

All of your categories should be profitable. Don't believe the old line: "If it doesn't sell now, it will sell at Christmas." Again, shopworn merch is like sour milk; people avoid it.

Merchandise Turn

Stocking the right amount of merch is an art. Purchase too much and you're stuck with lost profits; too little, and you're out of stock. You're going to lose out if a customer has to look elsewhere for the item.

Everyone joked when Starbucks opened several new shops close to existing locations. However, the company knew that 90 percent of Americans drink their coffee by 11 A.M. and that each person standing in front of one of its customers represented a minute wait. If someone looking to get a cup of coffee opened the door to Starbucks and encountered a line of 20 people, he would probably opt not to wait. But if he leaves and sees another Starbucks, the company still captures the sale because the product is available. Starbucks knew its customers; it did not want to be out of stock.

In his book, *Retail: The Art and Science* (2004), author Daniel Moe suggests that retailers organize their merchandise into four major roles: primary business drivers, traffic builders, profit generators, and impulse/add-ons. That way, you know the role each product will have in contributing to your sales.

For a grocery store it might look like:

Primary Business Driver (main category)	Staples like produce and meats
Traffic Driver (brings them in)	Commodities like soda, milk, eggs, diapers
Profit Generator	Deli, meal replacement, bakery
Impulse/Add-ons	Fresh flowers

For a bookstore it might look like:

Primary Business Driver	Hardcovers, bestsellers, paperbacks
Traffic Driver	New releases, coffeehouses
Profit Generator	Coffee table books, bargain books, DVDs
Impulse/Add-ons	Bookmarks, cards, stationery, gift wrap

By organizing your merchandise into categories, you can be sure you have filled the roles necessary to be profitable.

How to Increase Your Merchandise Turnover

1. Keep your bestsellers in stock by monitoring your POS category reports. Find the top five sellers within each category every week and balance to outstanding orders.

2. Before buying anything, make sure you know what it will replace. Impulse is for customers, not store buyers.

3. Come up with an optimal level of merchandise based on your POS reports, your merchandise turn, and profitability; then create your open-to-buy and buy to fill. This can be tricky if a category has very high- and/or low-priced items; in that case, split the category.

4. Watch your expected delivery dates. If you ordered merchandise meant to be sold together, remember to keep it together. You don't want its first appearance to be diluted. Later, the few items that may be left can be grouped with new arrivals to give them a new look. For example, if you ordered holiday candles from one vendor, mugs from another, and teas from another, wait for them all to arrive. Don't put the candles out first by themselves and lose the potential add-on sale. In that circumstance, simply taking a digital picture when you purchase them will serve as a reminder.

Average Sale

This is the most immediate report you can use to grow sales because it measures how well your sales crew can move your products. The more people like your employees, the more trust employees will be able to create and use to upsell each order. This is what raises your average sale. Every sector calls it something different, from an average ticket in a restaurant to the average daily rate in hotels. Whatever you call it, it is the closest we can get to knowing how much each customer purchased from you that day. Careful Analyticals, don't get caught up thinking of exceptions that can bring your average down, like ringing up a piece of candy versus your usual sale. Using your POS report averages everything so you have a true number to work with.

How to Increase Your Average Sale

1. Prioritize *sales*, not stocking. There is a saying in the restaurant business: "If you can lean, you can clean." In the retail

business, I think it should be, "If you can stock, you can sell." Too often we let employees think stocking the store shelves with product is more important than moving the product out the door. Displays are *supposed* to get messed up; products are *supposed* to look almost out. You have to explain this during employee training or your well-meaning staff members will fail you, especially Analyticals who are used to keeping order.

2. Hire more employees so there's an opportunity to upsell during busy times.

3. Increase add-on sales through impulse items displayed strategically around your store. (We'll cover that in more detail in the next chapter.)

4. Raise sales of higher-ticket goods by using features and benefits as well as add-ons through improved sales training. (We'll cover this extensively in Chapter 4.)

Average Number of Items

This is your total number of items sold divided by number of transactions. This is another way to track and measure how good a job your sales crew is doing and if your displays and signage are tempting customers to add on. The more items in every transaction, the more profit you will make. That's because it takes so much marketing money to capture a new customer (one client figured it at $247) that you only make profit on the second item, so your goal should always be for customers to buy more during a promotion. For example, employees should suggest during a storewide sale, "Since this is such a good price, how about getting two?" That simple offer builds the unit sales without adding any marketing costs. When you have trained salespeople, they can be focused on building the basket, the cart, or the bag with multiple items, which spreads out any discounts given over the more profitable add-ons. When you have clerks, customers will cherry-pick your best deals and leave with only one item.

How to Increase the Number of Items per Sale

1. Increase your point-of-purchase signage on higher profit items by stressing what the product will *do* for the customer not what it has.

2. Create a checklist to hand to customers to complete their purchase. A paint store, for instance, might have a flier titled, "Forget anything?" with a bulleted list including masking tape, razor blades, new roller, and so on that a cashier could ask a customer to look over. A florist could have something similar with a balloon, card, box of chocolates, and so on.

When I first began working with Marty Cox and his wife Louise Montgomery at It's A Grind Coffee House—their five-store, Long Beach, California-based chain—I made the case we had to come up with a premium line of specialty drinks that would lift the average check from $3.50 to over $4.25. They liked the idea, and we set about coming up with five premium drinks that the cashiers could upsell. These were not deals but distinct flavor profiles that also were very profitable because they were made from existing ingredients. In an interview with *Family Business* magazine, Marty attributes a good portion of the business's 28 percent increase in sales that year to such guidance. Because of that success, we came up with a limited-time-only promotion of super-premium drinks that rotated every 60 days, which became an integral part of building a nationwide franchised coffee chain of over 125 restaurants.

Franchise owner Tim McCabe shared his success with the premium menu items. "At my It's A Grind Coffee House in Galt, California, the limited-time premium drinks are a critical element in achieving my $5-plus average ticket per transaction. We are able to maintain the highest ticket average in the chain due to the emphasis on these exceptional drinks. My team members believe in promoting these drinks, as they know their customers will love them, and the added tips aren't bad, either! Our menu stays fresh and exciting, which drives sales and profit dollars, as well as increased return visits from our customers."

It's amazing what a simple menu/product/service change can do for business.

Average Number of Customers

Though often called a customer count, this is the total number of sales transactions. The recent recession has meant fewer customers for many businesses; but if we aren't tracking them, we may not be making every effort to encourage them to return. That's why I recommend looking at your monthly average number of customers and comparing it to at least the past three—or even better, five—years. Sometimes we think we're losing a lot of ground, when in fact, we're holding steady and may have even gained customers without knowing it. Looking at both this and your average transaction report over the past three years can show you how loyal your customers are, how effective your marketing is, and how much people want to shop with you.

Year–over–Year

Although you've already assessed your monthly sales, analyzing them over a period of three to five years helps even out the inconsistencies of times when holidays fall or weather impacts your area. Sometimes people panic when April Easter sales disappoint, only to realize the holiday was in March the previous year. It also helps you determine if a current year is an anomaly or part of a larger trend.

The Will to Change

In the past, you needed little preparation to get into business. All it took was an idea and the cash (or someone to loan you the cash), and poof!—you could be in business. It doesn't mean that you'd learned about it in business school or that you had the necessary tools, but overall, it was pretty easy. *Build it and they will come.* You might have felt as invincible as a 20-year-old driving a convertible.

Monitor Customers

Tip: If you want to get a good idea of just how well your products, displays, and salespeople are capturing customers' interest, monitor the people coming in and those who purchased. Take an hour; make a hashmark on a piece of paper for every person who comes in. For a family of five, make five marks. After the hour, note your conversion rate (the number of sales you made that hour divided into the number of customers who came in). You'll be able to show yourself and your crew there's probably a lot of room for improvement.

The past three years have clearly displayed the dangers of ignoring what happens when you don't pay attention to your business—especially for Feelers. People haven't just experienced declining profits and closed stores (although those are clearly dire outcomes); many have even lost their homes as a result. Others have been unable to make a profit and support a family, so owners take on other jobs to support their family business.

American family businesses must get back to basics and grow smarter about becoming profitable. The endless promotion of low-price and discounting that has eroded the businessman's reason to invest in America must be reversed. It hurts when I hear people say they don't take a salary from their family business. That means they have all of the problems but none of the financial rewards. The reason kids don't want to be a part of most family businesses is because they see all of the work and none of the benefits. It's akin to always having the baby in dirty diapers instead of seeing your child going off to college. It is therefore up to the older generation to fix their businesses if they want to pass them on to younger generations of family and employees.

While I was gathering information for the business makeover at Mike Sheldrake's Polly's Gourmet Coffee, I sat at a table within earshot of the counter. I watched a customer order a latte and a scone. The cashier rang up a latte for $2.75, and the customer handed her a $10 bill. From the change he received back from the cashier, the customer dropped a $5 bill in the tip jar and placed the rest in his pocket. This pattern continued throughout the morning. The complimentary scones from the cashier got her a wad of tips—but decreased the owner's bottom line.

At a meeting of all the employees later that week, I pointed to a picture of the *Titanic* and said, "Ladies and gentlemen, we're on this ship right now; and it's not going down on my watch. We're losing money hand over fist; and from this moment on the discounts and special favors are over." The free-scone-giving cashier immediately stood up crying and said—as she grabbed her backpack and headed for the door—"You can't treat us this way. I quit." But I continued, "I know you're stealing from Mike, and it ends today." I was intent upon shattering the easy street employment situation these employees had established—where they won and the business lost. Another girl got up and quit, and within 30 days, all but one were gone. Drivers are often the bearers of change needed to get results. Sales rose 11 percent for that month and (with major changes) went on to increase 50 percent year-over-year.

It is scary to have confrontational conversations, especially if you are an Amiable personality. But sometimes you have to pull the carrot out of the ground and examine the roots. That crew had created its own reality of five-finger discounts because there was no training program, there were no standards, and Mike was not looking at the most important thing: a profit. A Feeler, he simply wanted to be liked.

Don't get stuck on the wrong stuff. Focus on what really matters: your sales skills and your ability to manage an open-to-buy and bring in a profit. And don't be a hypochondriac who makes out everything about your business to be terrible; nothing is ever *that* bad. When I asked one particular mentee of mine for his sales reports, he would preface them by saying, "If it weren't for that big sale, it would have been a terrible month." I replied, "Yeah, but you *had* that big sale." "Well," he said, "It's been dead here lately. Nobody's coming in." I then asked, "So how much are you down?" "About 9 percent." I told him, "Well then, *somebody* is coming in."

Wherever you are with your business, today is a new day. Maybe you are doing great and looking to improve; maybe you have started doing the wrong things like leaving the store to pick up your kids then not returning as scheduled, hiring friends, and holding lots of sales because you're scared. Or maybe you just purchased a business and have never had to run one by yourself. It doesn't matter how you got here; we're going to make it better.

STAT: Five Things to Do Immediately after Reading This Chapter

1. Schedule your top five reports to be e-mailed to you every Monday morning.
2. Compare your busiest times for the past three weeks to effectively schedule and maximize your coverage.
3. Review your average check and develop a plan to increase it by 10 percent.
4. Track your number of units per transaction to give clues as to your crew's ability to upsell.
5. Track your customer counts for the past three weeks to see if you are getting more out of those who stop in your store.

If you are looking to get even more out of this book, you may be interested in a special program I have that includes all the spreadsheets you need, mystery shops, and a consultation with me. Look for details at the end of the book or at www .retaildoc.com/guide/update.php.

Chapter 2

The Anatomy of a Successful Retail Store

Much like an allergist analyzes the surroundings in your home to find the cause of your symptoms, we now aim to see how the physical stuff of your store—your four walls and the contents therein—affects your business's health. Dust, disorganization, and poor displays won't kill you, but they are reliable indications that your business is not running very well. We'll discover how important merchandising, maintenance, and movement are to a successful store. You'll learn my 11 tips to make your store look bigger as well as some of the common mistakes businesses make.

I read a newspaper article back in 1997 about how a Starbucks was about to open only 75 feet from the front door Polly's Gourmet Coffee in Long Beach, California. Since 1976, Polly's had had a reputation for having the best fresh roasted coffee in town. They were so far ahead of the curve that they didn't even know they were trendsetters. I had read the editorials and letters to the editor about how big bad corporate coffee purveyor Starbucks was trying to put yet another little independent out of business. So one Saturday, I invited a friend of mine to meet me for coffee. I had to see this place for myself.

As I drove up to the shop at the end of the popular shopping district on a Saturday night, I noticed that half of the parking lot lights were out. The front door was missing paint, the patio was dirty, the neon sign was dark, the patio was strewn with discarded newspapers, and the planter boxes were filled with weeds and cigarette butts. I assumed that the shop was closing as I walked in—even though it was only 6 P.M.—

because a majority of the light fixtures were burnt out, leaving very little light in the coffeehouse. The two employees were talking to each other as I scanned the cedar wood walls and the ceiling that held stains from leaks in the roof and smoke from the coffee roaster.

The merchandise—including a coffeemaker with a sign for $300 dollars—had a half-inch layer of dust on them. I picked up a coffee mug that—like the other items on the half-empty shelf—had no price tag on it. The condiment bar was sloppy, covered with spilt milk and sugar packets. But that wasn't the worst part; the employees kept talking as I approached the counter.

"When that new Starbucks comes in, he'll never survive," said one. I waited at the counter. The other employee added, "Yeah, I've already got my application into three other places saying I was the manager—I figured no one will check." I interrupted them to order a cappuccino and a latte.

From the dirt and lack of maintenance of the coffeehouse to his employees' clear lack of confidence in him, this owner was telegraphing the fact that he was in trouble to all who visited his business. *Could that be you right now?*

Great retail mimics the best qualities of our homes. When you create a comfortable space in which people enjoy spending time, they change from mission shoppers looking for one item to profitable browsers who buy more. To see what I mean, visit some of the beautifully designed retailers in your local mall like Crate & Barrel, Restoration Hardware, or Williams-Sonoma, and you'll find an idealized home. They are clean and bright with areas of discovery, places in which you'd be happy to linger for a while. These stores are masters at showcasing various items in coordinated settings that make the shopper notice and consider taking them home to enjoy. Your first job in growing your business is making your store as compelling as that of any competitor.

Sadly, this is frequently where many businesses fall down, because no one is looking at how the stage is set to welcome customers. That continues when employees get away with murder by standing behind the counter with their heads lying on their outstretched arms moaning, "It's so *dead.*" Even in a doctor's, accountant's, or a lawyer's office, the rules of hospitality prepare the customer for a great—or not-so-great—

experience. These are situations in which we truly judge a book by its cover because a customer never forgets how you made them feel.

How well your store or showroom is cleaned and organized signals a welcoming sign to customers that things are going well—or a warning sign that you're in trouble.

I was watching a recent Yankees game during which announcer Michael Kay commented about the Rogers Center, the home of the Toronto Blue Jays. The camera zoomed around and found that "B" and "u" were missing on the sign, which then read the "l e Jays." Fellow announcer David Cone recalled aloud having played for the Blue Jays when the stadium was new in 1989 and referenced the fact that the Jays attracted a record 4-million-plus fans that year. But that night, the ballpark was less than half full. People notice when you take your eyes off the ball, so create a plan to ensure standards are met.

The following sections might seem like the basics Feelers, but you have to *prepare* for any displaying of your merchandise. You begin this with a grid of your floor plan.

The Grid

Because you can't close down to renovate, one way to refresh your store is to divide it into nine sections like a tic-tac-toe board. Beginning at the front by your door, number each section (see Figure 2.1).

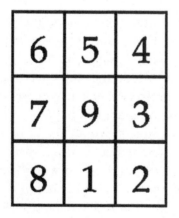

FIGURE **2.1**   Segment Your Store into a Grid

Then:

◆ Strip everything off the shelves, the floor, the fixtures, the ceiling. Don't cut corners.

◆ Clean everything as you take it off. Cellophane on a box a bit yellow? Put it in the back marked "sale." Shirts too dirty on one sleeve from being on a rounder too long? Mark them down. If you're a shoe store, match display units with the mate in the back. After a thorough attempt to match any mismatches, rip out the label and use a hole punch to mark the leftovers so you can donate to a charity and write off. (If you just throw them out, someone could bring them back in without a receipt looking for an exchange. If you destroy them with boxcutters, like H&M did in Manhattan and you're caught, you could provoke an outrage.)

◆ Price everything. If something has gone up in price, make sure that the new price is marked. If you no longer carry an item, put it in the back on sale. Put a date on all nonsale items in order to mark down more efficiently going forward.

◆ Clean the walls of any leftover tape, pushpins, or nails.

◆ Replace all lightbulbs that are burned out.

◆ Paint any walls that need freshening up; use wood cleaner on your slat walls; clean all rounders and racks with furniture polish so items move easier for browsing; and take packing tape to the corners of the carpets to get rid of the dust.

Work on this grid until you've done the whole store. Clean the carpets if you are able. Then come up with a daily checklist to maintain cleanliness. Not sure what to put on it? Work backward. Look at what you just cleaned and include the steps necessary to keep that from becoming a major project. You'll use these checklists when you develop your training program in Chapter 4.

Next, notice your store's overall smell. Is it overpowering with incense, fragrant candles, or other perfume-y smells? If so, people with sensitive noses might bolt for the door with their one item. If it smells old, musky, or dusty, it won't inspire shoppers. Remember, the best stores are like our homes: neat, clean, and well-organized.

The last thing you use to create the feeling of home is the music you choose for ambient sound in your store, restaurant, or other business. This can affect how long customers want to stay or how quickly they leave. Experiment with classical, light pop, or instrumental for a week at a time; see if your customers browse longer and if your average sales grow with each type and adopt whichever produces the greatest results.

Traffic Flow

Now that we have a clean slate, we have to think about how traffic flows through your store. I've noticed when customers in North America enter a store, they move to the right, continuing counter-clockwise until they leave (see Figure 2.2).

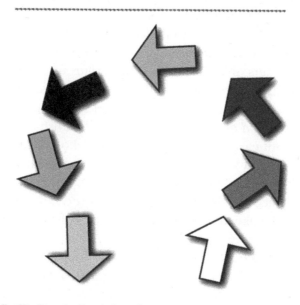

FIGURE 2.2   Traffic Flow in North America

Most of your profitable sales will come from the first third of your store, so merchandising around your traffic flow is essential. You want the premium, most exciting items—the *wants*—at the front of the store as customers walk in. Putting the needs, the things people have to have, in the back works for grocery stores and retailers alike.

However, putting all of your leftovers, clearance sale has-beens, or other junk up at the front hoping they'll entice somebody is like walking into somebody's living room and finding a garage sale. Copy the setup of clothing retailer The Gap and put the sale stuff in the back. I guarantee that bargain shoppers will find them.

Remember as well that you don't want your best products on the left side of the store, because after someone has paid for her merchandise, where are her eyes? Straight ahead, looking for the door, oblivious to even the best display. This is *never* where we want customers to look.

Use the Arrow Floor Design to Avoid Church Aisle Layouts

When you walk into most any church or synagogue, you notice that all of the pews are at right angles, forcing you to look straight up to the altar. You aren't supposed to notice who is beside you; you are to concentrate solely on the front.

Many retailers unknowingly set their stores up in much the same way by having one central aisle that leads to a cash register. When someone does look down a side aisle, he or she is typically looking at the wall *at the end of the aisle*, not the merchandise *in the aisle*. This layout makes it easy for Driver or Analytical shoppers to walk in the door, look straight ahead, and maybe a little bit to the right and left. They quickly "get it," lose interest, and bolt for the door. That's why we want to place your display units at a 45-degree angle off your main aisle. Think of it like the end of an arrow where the feathers go off at a 45-degree angle (see Figure 2.3).

When customers encounter the arrow floor design, they see all the endcaps, which, when displayed properly, make them stop and discover what else you have down that aisle.

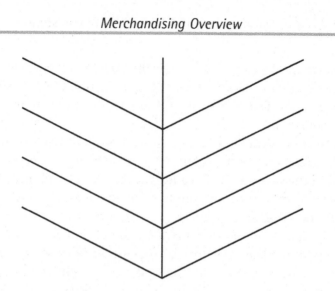

FIGURE **2.3**   Organize Racks Like the Tail of an Arrow

Merchandising Overview

Merchandising is how you showcase your products in your store. Some stores only display using the old retail mantra: "Stack it high and watch it fly." After all, that works for the big boys, right?

Yes, it works for mass merchants like Wal-Mart and Target that sell a lot of merch at a low price; they make their money on the high volume of units sold. Independents, however, sell far less than these big name retailers; therefore, you have to get more profit out of each transaction. A well thought-out display can help you increase your conversion rate (the number of customers who purchased as a percentage of people who visited your store) because—like an employee who is always pitching the add-on—the display is your silent salesperson.

I'm always amazed when I hear from store owners that their conversion rate is "around 80 percent"—only to do an audit for them and find that it's more like 20 percent. Know what this number is and know how to make it better!

A great display takes customers from either not noticing or feeling stupid after noticing a product, to giving them a clear picture of how it would look in their homes, how they could use it in their businesses, or how they could combine several items. Great displays help build sales because they stop customers in their tracks and persuade them to select an item they hadn't necessarily considered. Conversely, sloppy or poorly coordinated displays rob your store of its ability to make additional profit.

I saw an endcap at a Ralph's grocery store in California that had Oreos, toilet paper, and bleach. *What in the world was the store trying to sell?* Nothing—exactly! Because nothing went with anything else. You never want a customer, like an Analytical, to scratch his head or an Amiable pointing and laughing to her girlfriend trying to figure out why your items are displayed in the manner they are.

Keep in mind, as well, that a large display of product rarely helps conversion rates. Picture an appliance store with row after row of refrigerators, washers, and dryers. What message stands out? The store has a lot of appliances. Without highlighting a specific item, you risk having your customers—especially Feeler personalities—get so overwhelmed and say to you as they are walking out the front door, "I'll have to think about it." Notice this week how many stores stack individual products, as the big boxes do with no signage. Nothing to draw our attention to certain features and benefits. Nothing that explains why the product might be just right for you—just piles of stuff. Period. That's because merchandising skills have fallen off a cliff the last 25 years.

The thing that makes specialty retail work is the *discovery* aspect. That's why your store displays have to be laid out in such a fashion that relationships are obvious to those who don't know your merch. The higher priced or more profitable items need help in a crowded store. They often have to go it alone as employees are rarely there at the moment of discovery and decision to convince the customer to pay full price. And just sticking a price in front of an item does nothing to enhance its value. You need to find ways to excite. For example, "Our best-selling scooter, indestructible, balanced, and lightweight, now comes in electric red."

Who is the most likely to excel at creating displays? The Expressives, because they naturally consider all choices. If this is not you, find someone on your team who is because they will enjoy this process. If you are the Expressive be aware, this is something you will naturally enjoy. Don't get so wrapped up in making great displays that you forget there are customers in your store needing to be sold your merch.

Segmenting Merchandise Lowers Sales

Some department stores still put all their women's tops in one section, all the jeans in another, all their sweaters in another, and so on. They don't realize that by doing so, they're cutting off their ability to grow sales. Why? Because there are no add-ons. Customers who were looking for jeans found them, tried them on, and took them to the counter where the employee asked, "Anything else?" And of course the answer was "No," because the customer didn't see anything else.

Merchandise your store like it's a world of choices, and you'll have a reason later on to do a store tour. (I'll talk about that in Chapter 3 as a way of getting your employees to help grow your conversion rate as well.)

Selecting the Merch for a Display

The following five questions can help you decide what to highlight:

1. Is it high profit? Even if it's something that has a medium price tag, can it deliver more profit if you pull it off the shelf and feature it?
2. Is it a limited-time item that can only sell for a short period? Something that's only available for a holiday loses value every day closer to the event, because it has a finite appeal.
3. Is it a want, in other words, an item that a customer might covet in his heart of hearts? For example, you want the contractor who goes in just to replace his drill bits to spot a display of your new stainless steel cordless drills and realize that he just *has* to have one.
4. Is it something that can be bundled? For example, a beauty salon could amass an assortment of products to deal with "frizziness," including the conditioning shampoo, hot oil conditioner, mousse for styling, and the hair dryer to minimize split

ends with a sign that says: "Finally, the system that conquers your split ends."

5. Is it inexpensive? The last thing we want to do is merchandise by discount; but it's the number-one way people display. The danger with that is that you draw attention to something that you may not make a lot of profit on.

A great store display has the power to persuade customers to consider purchasing more than they initially planned. Figure 2.4 shows a display from the Sur La Table store in Glendale, California, which ties

FIGURE 2.4   A Summer BBQ Display at Sur La Table

all of the various departments in the store into one barbeque display for summer.

It's less work to create one of the following types of displays, which will also help move product.

The Eight Types of Displays

1. **Complementary displays** say, "This makes this better." For example, you often find the *Eggo* maple syrup displayed on the freezer door to the product in the waffles section of the frozen food aisle (see Figure 2.5). You might also see the shortcake displayed next to the strawberries in the fresh fruit aisle, or the chips by the margarita mix in a liquor aisle. A hardware store's picture hanger display might include a small hammer, wire,

FIGURE **2.5**   A Display on a Freezer Door; Maple Syrup Complements the Frozen Waffles

and a stud finder. These are all methods of completing the picture to show customers that *this* goes with—and would be even better with—*this*.

2. **Coordinated displays** say, "These are all the items you need for this to work." For example, a department store would display women's slacks on a four-way fixture with the coordinated tops that go with the matching bag that goes with the jewelry shown in the middle of the display unit. A linen store might exhibit the bath towel in blue that goes with the yellow and blue stripe washcloth, which goes with the blue stripe towel holder, which goes with the coordinating cup and Q-tips holder (see Figure 2.6).

   A camera store would want to combine a digital camera, photo printer, and the accompanying photo paper. In a furniture store, we might find the safari artwork that goes with the

FIGURE **2.6**   A Display at a Linen Store

FIGURE **2.7**   A Display at a Scrapbook Store

dark wood and brass chest that matches the giraffe print sofa and overstuffed zebra pillows all in shades of taupe and brown. A scrapbook store might have the gold stickers that go with the frame that complements the sepia historical photos that corresponds to the miniature map of California that matches the alphabet buttons, so that we see the whole picture when we look at the display—not just aisles of each individual item (see Figure 2.7).

3. **Displays of the same product** arranged altogether can make a big impact. For example, a Ralph's grocery store had nothing but gourds and pumpkins in one display to either side of the front doors during the fall (see Figure 2.8 on the top of the following page). An office supply store had a display of the same binder that showed all the different colors it came in.

4. **Environmental displays** show the product in use. What truly makes these exhibits are the oversize graphics or props; that's how you know that you're looking at one. A garden center could set up the pesticide aisle to display pictures of the most common pests with the product to get rid of them lined up underneath (see Figure 2.9 on the following page).

FIGURE **2.8**   A Display of Gourds and Pumpkins at Ralph's

FIGURE **2.9**   A Pesticide Display

There is a great wine store in New York City called Bottlerocket Wine and Spirit that has several display units in the middle of the store (see Figure 2.10 on the following page). On the top middle of each is a different type of food that one might eat with wine. One says, "Take-out," with a large white Chinese takeout box. Underneath it at various heights are all the wines

FIGURE 2.10   Display Units at Bottlerocket Wine and Spirit

that go with takeout foods like pizza and barbeque. The next display back has a giant salmon on top and a sign that reads, "Seafood." This continues with a "Recipes" display that exhibits all sorts of cookbooks, and then "Dessert." Shoppers are able to get the idea quickly without having to ask somebody, "What would go with this?" No wonder they have a patent pending on this business model. Unlike in a typical wine store, these display units do the heavy lifting of piquing the customer's interest *before* it is matched with the excitement of a well-trained employee.

Major appliance retailer Whirlpool established its Insperience Studio near Atlanta, Georgia, in 2003. The studio provided a live, hands-on environment where consumers could experience some of Whirlpool's brands—including Kitchen-Aid, Maytag, and Jenn-Air—before committing to purchase. Instead of just looking at a store display, customers first encountered the products in an actual home setting where they could try, pick up, and even bring their own food and laundry in to "try before you buy." Similarly, Hunter Douglas Window Fashions Gallery dealers each invest nearly $45,000 into full-size working displays of every blind and shade the company makes to show an environment that's most like a customer's own home.

Environmental displays tend to be more permanent in nature and have the ability to grab customers' attention quickly. However, they do take up more space in your windows or on your sales floor.

5. **Side-out or face-out displays** present the merchandise in a more complete way. Consider walking into a bookstore where all you see are the spines of the books; it would be impossible to make a selection. Barnes & Noble and Borders both broke ground when they offered more display space to face-out titles. Sales skyrocketed, because people really see the cover.

Consider entering two types of motorcycle dealerships: one where all the bikes are inches away from each other, and one where there are four or five feet between them. In the first, you look at the display of headlights and nothing stands out (see Figure 2.11). In the second, the space allows you to see the whole side of the vehicle, picture yourself on it, and take your time to discover it (see Figure 2.12). Look for this more and more in grocery stores as they expand face-out merchandising, so you are not noticing the shelf but the product. That is the hallmark of this type of display.

6. **Stop displays** are totally unrelated to your product or even your business. I often refer to this as the "pig in the window" display. I learned many years ago from author Peter Glen to put one seemingly irrelevant item in the window. For example, including a small plush toy pig in a home furnishings store display grabs customers' attention and makes them wonder why you included it. A lighting store window with 50 light bulbs all hanging from the exact same color cord and fixture with only one lit will incite curiosity. That makes us Thinkers wonder, "Why?" That's the gist of this type of display.

FIGURE 2.11   The First Display at a Motorcycle Dealership

FIGURE 2.12   The Second Display of a Star Raider at a Yamaha Motorcycle Dealership

FIGURE **2.13**   A Picture Framing Shop window in Paris, France

7. **Using your product as art**—or, in any new and unusual way—attracts customer interest. An optical shop in Portland, Oregon, took four umbrellas and suspended them as if someone were holding them up. The shop took various lenses and using fishing wire attached them, so it looked like it was raining.

I walked past the window of a picture frame shop in Paris with five frames—each bigger than the next—displaying actual loaves of bread (see Figure 2.13). At first, I wasn't sure what I was looking at because it was three-dimensional. These are some of the hardest types of displays to pull off, but if you've been doing displays for awhile, this might give you a burst of inspiration.

8. **Teaching display.** This compares features and benefits to help the customer choose the right product out of a seemingly endless number of choices. Amiables and Expressives respond to this because it helps them avoid being overloaded, so they purchase instead of walk past. For example, the Staples display of papers (shown in Figure 2.14) teaches you the difference between the various types, much like a salesperson would.

FIGURE **2.14** A Teaching Display of Papers

Each of these displays has its place; my goal in identifying each kind is to help you see all the options you have to be creative and catch the customer's attention. And don't forget that the granddaddy of displays is windows. If you have foot traffic that can stop and be drawn in, all eight types of displays can be used effectively to grow your walk-ins.

Now that we know where, how, and what kind of display to make—how will you build it?

How to Merchandise Your Store
1. **Put new arrivals first.** As previously mentioned, if you ordered merchandise meant to go together, keep it together. You don't want its first appearance to be diluted. Later, the few

items that may be left can be grouped with new arrivals to give them a new look.

2. **Group items together.** Look for one thing that makes a group and creates the best add-on sale you can come up. For example: flowers, corresponding thank-you notes, a flower print pen, and a matching balloon. All of one product works well in a grocery store, but it is little more than warehousing the items in a retail store.

3. **Inventory what you have to work with.** While you *can* feature one-of-a-kind items, you generally don't want to, because your display is ruined once one sells.

4. **Use contrasting colors.** The strongest color combinations to attract attention in retail are red, white, and black.

5. **Vary heights to add interest.** You can see in the grocery store example in Figure 2.15 how the different heights of onions and potatoes drew attention to the various sizes and made walking in past them more inviting.

6. **Light your display like it's show time.** Light makes the merchandise pop, so adjust overheard lighting. If you have a particularly dark display with no way to light it from above, consider moving it to an existing light source or highlight it from below with small spotlights.

7. **Add well-placed signs.** Make sure they are worded clearly, short and easy to read, and make benefits—not just a price or discount—obvious to the customer. Keep in mind that America is aging; so don't use too small a type font.

8. **Treat endcaps as display units.** Moving a product from its regular shelf location to a featured endcap has been proven to lead to an average sales increase of 25 percent during the test period. If you display more than one product on an endcap, make sure they are related items. All things relating to camping, for example, will work but a canteen, oil filter, and a lawn sprinkler—not so much.

9. **Keep it simple.** Don't group more than three different products together. We're pressed for time so make it easy for us to scan.

Figure 2.15 Different Heights Add Interest

10. **Keep your display stocked but not too full.** You want it to look like people are buying your merchandise and that it is popular. Make sure to train your Analytical staff on this point or it will, by nature, want to keep everything stocked to the gills.

11. **Clean and dust your displays regularly so they shine.** Consider doing this several times a day.

12. **Change your display every two weeks.** Move existing displays around in the store when new merchandise comes in. Since the fairly new products will still be selling, switch your displays two weeks after their arrival. Move one display from the front to the middle of the store and the other from the middle to the back.

13. **Monitor your computer printouts and inventory levels weekly.** Be prepared to reorder immediately if something really takes off. If you have sold through your inventory and you have no back stock, change the display to something you have plenty of. If something doesn't sell, try moving the display to another location before giving up on it.

14. **Price everything.** No one wants to have to ask how much something is.

Four Merchandising Don'ts

1. Don't display just one color; the mind gets used to it and moves on. Mix at least two; three is better for maximum impact.

2. Don't put up a sign that says DO NOT TOUCH (Analyticals!). You might as well put up a sign that says DO NOT BUY. Displays are *supposed* to get messed up. Remember: Our goal is to welcome customers like guests to our home. That means that we treat them like we *want* them there, not as though they're gatecrashers.

3. Don't put *want* items lower than 24 inches off the floor or higher than eye level—they will not sell. Put the needs below and above, because people will look for them.

4. Don't merchandise your entire store by product type. These kinds of displays encourage mission shoppers like Drivers and Analyticals who are looking for one item. Since they don't tell a story, they don't promote browsing. Wine stores tend to do this, which is dangerous because in a world of choice, customers (especially the Feelers) frequently don't know what the right choice is. Because displays of hundreds of red wines do not help them make an intelligent choice for their needs, customers' eyes glaze over, they get overwhelmed, the "idiot switch" is tripped, they shut down and either choose an old standby they've had before, select by price, or walk.

Avoid Unwelcoming Signs

We often see signs like "No food or drink," or "Children must be accompanied by an adult"—things that tell people to stay out. Most standoffish signs come from people who do not want to be bothered. They think that putting a rule in writing will take care of the problem—which it rarely does. One library I worked with on a makeover had nearly a dozen signs taped to the entrance doors. Any guesses which personality type tends to use these signs? You're right—Analyticals.

The unwelcoming attitude frequently shows up in unexpected places, like curb signs that say, "Walk-ins welcome as time permits," or signs at the register including, "Hang up your cell phones before ordering," or "Present coupons before ordering or they will not be honored."

The unwelcoming attitude continues with signs over tables: "No table saving," or at the free breakfast at a hotel: "One serving of bread per guest." To grow your sales, you need to put out the red carpet not the red flag.

Now that you've created displays inside your store to add interest—how about the outside? Here are several ideas you can implement to stop customers from driving by.

12 Ways to Make Your Store Look Bigger

1. **Product.** If you have large enough products, wheel your *best* one in front of your store every day. If you're a motorcycle dealer, I know, they're heavy—so what? Nothing grabs speeding customers' eyes faster than a shiny new vehicle. It says that you are the source for excitement. Vary it depending on season. Afraid of the weather? Put a portable canopy over it. If you're an apparel store, probably not worth it; but a plant nursery—you bet.

2. **Standout displays** say, "Made you look!" For example, a bicycle dealer that puts a bike on top of its building; a coffee-house with an inflatable coffee cup on the top of the awning; a window treatment store with actual draperies on the outside of its building—all are examples of this type of the display, and ways to represent what the merchant carries. My client Aron

Lieberman, found he could really draw attention to his business when we made it look like draperies were hanging on the outside of his historic home showroom. (See Figure 2.16).

3. **Light pole signs.** You've seen these at gas stations and fast-food restaurants. They are about four feet by six feet, made of a durable synthetic, and are attached to the light poles by cable ties. These should be printed in full color—maybe a red loveseat with "Valentine's Day Is Coming!" and your logo at the bottom for January. Speak with your landlord to see if there is any objection. Put one sign up on the side that faces the most traffic and another on the other side of the pole. The goal with these types of signs is not to sell anything (Big Sale 20% Off!), but to showcase your best product. Think of something short like, "Learn to Ride" for a motorcycle dealer, "The Perfect Birthday" for a party store, or "You *Can* Cook" for either an organic grocery or cooking supply store.

FIGURE **2.16**   Rockland Window Coverings, Spring Valley, NY

4. **Flags.** An inexpensive option is to string pennant flags from a light pole to the front of your business. You can get a multicolor version at sporting goods stores for under $50. The trick with flags is to replace them about every other month while they are still bright and before they are all ripped.

5. **Building banners.** Particularly in new developments, you may have a very generic building wall. Consider a tall banner from roof to sidewalk in eye-catching but not garish colors; think forest instead of fluorescent green. Write something at the top like, "We've got" and add pictures of your best products. Again, the goal is not to scream price but to showcase the *wants*. See if your vendors would co-op to save money. City sign ordinances might seem to prohibit such banners, but check; they will usually let you have it up for 90 days.

6. **Wicket signs.** These are lightweight signs often used by realtors for open houses because of their reasonable cost (less than $30 each) to grab motorists' attention. They are pushed into the ground and stand approximately three feet high by two feet wide. These might be a good choice for a limited-time promotion for getting your message out into your parking lot or by the median of a busy intersection. The example shown in Figure 2.17 on the following page encourages customers to shop the dealership online. While some are sturdier than others, they do not take much wind. Again, keep them simple with large fonts. Even if your city has sign police, these can generally be used on weekends when they're off duty.

7. **Floor banners.** These are placed outside in situations where you cannot use a building banner but want to convey the same message. The cost, with a weighted banner holder, can be a couple hundred dollars; the banner can be changed monthly to refresh your image.

8. **Curb signs.** Using a professional curb sign like the MDI WindMaster gives your store's message a professional look. Weatherproof, with a base you can fill with sand, water, or anti-freeze, it will last for years (see Figure 2.18 on page 47). For about $300, you can use this important tool for high-quality

FIGURE 2.17   A Wicket Sign in Columbia, CT

color graphics to stand out from your competitors who write a generic "Sale."

9. **Inflatables.** This is a fairly expensive item ($3,000 to $4,000 for a custom unit); but if your city has no objections, it could provide instant recognition for your business. The downside is that while generic ones like a gorilla or other character may get noticed, customers may not go much further than to say, "Hey, there's a gorilla over there," and move on.

10. **Monument sign.** While these can be expensive (a onetime cost of $2,000 to $10,000 paid to your landlord), they do let potential customers speeding by know your business is one of those in the center.

11. **Landscaping.** One of the most successful chain restaurants is Mimi's Café that spends very little on ads. What they do is put a lot of money toward the landscaping around their restaurants;

FIGURE 2.18 A Curb Sign

there is not a patch of earth that is not blooming throughout much of the year. Why do they do this? Because the restaurant knows its abundance of flowers will attract customers' eyes, so everyone knows its location in town. If you have nothing but sidewalks in front of you, plant up some large pots—either on the ground or off the supports—with something like bright red geraniums. Keep them watered, fed, and well maintained. In the winter, plant junipers and string lights on them. I can hear some of you thinking, "Guys won't appreciate that." But remember that guys are often the ones maintaining their own yards.

12. **Balloons.** There's nothing cheaper that provides movement and attention to your business. If you have a railing, use that. If you have nowhere to tie them to, you can lay cinderblocks flat and tie the strings through the holes. Use them for a special event like a grand opening, and be sure to use plenty and replace often as helium deflates in the sun.

One more thought: Make sure that you have your parking lot patched and sealed annually. You must look new and successful, not old and struggling. When you make yourself look bigger and feature our *wants*, you'll pique our interest in what you have waiting inside.

Ways to Look Unsuccessful

1. Nothing appears more desperate than a person standing on the sidewalk holding a red arrow pointing to your business. Though it may get you attention, it just makes people think: "poor guy." (If your store is that hidden, you should have thought of that before you opened. I don't care what the traffic count is, you don't want to be 100 feet from success.) The people chosen for arrow duty are typically the saddest-looking people, bored, headphones in their ears and their eyes staring vacantly into traffic—oftentimes with a cheap beach chair by their side. And it's even worse to use your own kids. Is this the image you want for your business? *No.*

2. Don't stick your old sale merchandise out onto the sidewalk. It looks like a garage sale. Those driving past will judge you by the way in which you've chosen to represent your business out front—by the junk no one wanted that you put on sale.

How to Get Rid of the Old Stuff

As you remerchandise your store, you'll invariably find product that isn't making you money. It could be product that's mostly sold through, been discontinued, or that no one wanted. Recheck every shelf, rack, display, as well as your stockroom and storage yard; and bring these items to your stockroom. Have someone clean all of them (unless it's clothing). If the items were previously on hangers, take them off and fold them on the table. If they were on a table, hang them all up. Create a sale tag for them with three elements:

1. The sale price
2. Percentage savings
3. The original price

For example: on a pair of shoes, "Sale $59.99, you save 40%, regularly $110." This gives a customer a good idea of the value of your clearance item. Start at 50 percent off if the stuff is old; don't tiptoe around getting rid of it. After two weeks, go to 60 percent for a week. If it doesn't sell by then, donate to a customer, employee, or charity. The clearance sale is intended to do just that: *clear out* the old to pay for the new. If you keep clearance items too long, they become distressed goods, which no one wants. Look at holiday 2008 when retailers were running 60, 70, and 80 percent off retail; it still didn't move the merch.

Don't wait for the day of the holiday to discount if you have holiday-themed items, If, for instance, you have Christmas sweaters that haven't sold by December 12, put them on sale and be out of them by Christmas Eve. If you have everything for a great backyard barbecue, put it on sale in mid-August and be sold out before Labor Day. Many businesses wait too long to take a discount and start at too little a discount to move the merchandise. Then when these items don't sell, they box them back up and put them in a warehouse somewhere where they might be soiled, broken, or forgotten. If items didn't sell this year, they probably won't next year either, so don't waste your money. I know, you thought it was so cute at the gift show, but, unfortunately, your customers didn't. Don't take it personally, Feelers; the fact that it didn't move doesn't say anything about *you.*

I was keynoting at an American Specialty Toy Retailing Association meeting in 2008, and a woman asked me how long to keep clearance merchandise. I told her my guidelines above and she said, "But I just know they'll sell eventually." Maybe so, but not at full price after nine months. Move on and aggressively clear out your stock on a regular basis—not just when you need money.

Once you take care of the store, both inside and out, you're ready to tackle the people. This could truly be both one of the most rewarding and frustrating opportunities to grow your business.

STAT: Six Things to Do Immediately after Reading This Chapter

1. Clean and price everything.
2. Create a grid to create and update displays.
3. Build a display with only a couple colors, related items at different heights, with signage, and light it.
4. Choose one thing to make your store look bigger and attract passersby.
5. Clear out or throw out the junk.
6. If you didn't take the personality test in the Introduction, please go back and do it before proceeding to get the most out of the rest of the book.

Chapter 3

The Right Employees Are Your Most Important Asset—How to Hire Right

Most people are unaware that their lungs have lots of little air pockets—each of which participates in your breathing. When some don't work right, the rest have to work harder—and that's when you find yourself gasping for air. Disease strikes when the lungs are unable to process air. The same thing happens with a bad hire. It's always hard to find good help, I understand. But you can't afford to settle for someone who can simply fill a shift.

This section looks at how to make sure a new employee contributes to your overall good health instead of making you gasp. We'll consider a variety of elements that are involved in getting the right person on your team, along with some questions you may never have considered. Here's a brief summary.

Before You Hire Anyone, You Must:
◆ Know what you want an employee to do, make sure you have a job description that covers everything.
◆ Know what you want in a great employee before you ever post the "Now Hiring" sign.
◆ Be aware of the nine points to cover when reviewing a job application—including previous experience, gaps in employment, and lack of previous experience.

When Recruiting

◆ Locate five places to find good prospects for your business.

◆ Find people interested in meeting other people who are friendly and have a welcoming attitude. If it were a dog park, you'd be looking for the Labradors not the Poodles. They can possess any of the four personalities; we'll cover the good and bad of each.

◆ Display entertaining signage that attracts fun people to work for you.

During the Process

◆ Know how to run a successful interview, the proper questions to ask, as well as the "A" answers you want to hear.

◆ Ask for specific past behavior to predict future behavior.

◆ Avoid hypothetical questions that begin, "What would you do . . . ?" or "Where do you think . . . ?"

◆ Discover which of the four personalities the candidate possesses.

When Deciding Who to Hire

◆ Check references.

◆ Recognize deal killers.

◆ Hire like you're casting characters for a movie.

◆ Hire the hungry not the starved.

Hiring is something that many managers view as a necessary evil—something to get over with, that solves a problem, and that, once done, completely absolves them from responsibility. Nothing could be further from the truth.

Why You Need Job Descriptions

Your job description is a tool you use to train, evaluate performance, and promote or remove an employee. A well-written job description can also protect you in the extreme situation of a court trial by showing why you chose to hire one person over another. Your goal is to create a balanced job description that sets expectations with responsibilities. It allows employees to know where one person's job leaves off and another's picks up, along with any prerequisites for a position.

Many businesses have tribal knowledge of what a job entails; employees have simply learned by doing. Polly's Gourmet Coffee owner (and Amiable) Mike Sheldrake used to have employees shadow each other to learn the business—until the day that an employee approached him and asked, "Can I take six pounds of coffee today, since I didn't take my free pound for the past six months?" He asked her where she had heard that. She replied, "What do you mean? Everyone understands you get a free pound of coffee each month." He never had such a program, and it made him wonder what else was going on based on his employees' "understanding."

Businesses tend to fall into two different camps when it comes to establishing written job descriptions. The first group has nothing written down, which I generally see with Feeler personalities. This makes it next to impossible to reprimand anyone for not performing at an acceptable level because no boundaries have been set. And because there is nothing to hold them accountable to, the employees generally are never reviewed. The second type of business has *everything* written into the job description—from procedures, policies, and expectations, to where employees should go to take a break, how to call in sick, and when to call a manager. I generally see this with owners who are Thinker personalities. These job descriptions are often pages long, rarely looked at, and so detailed that they are impractical at best—and a complete waste of time.

How to Create Your Job Descriptions

Take out a piece of paper and write down what an employee does. Don't make any judgments; just write down the tasks. If you want, ask your current employees to write down what they do. Your goal is to agree to the scope of the job and responsibilities. Once you're done, group these items into three categories: essential functions, physical demands, and skills. Next, consider whether there is required knowledge, education, or experience necessary for anyone holding this job. Write your job description with a general paragraph at the top and essential functions below. Include a signature line at the bottom so that when you hire for the position, the person who takes it can acknowledge his understanding of what the job entails. See the example in Figure 3.1.

Most businesses will need a trainee job description, assistant manager, and manager job description; and the higher the title, the more general the explanation of responsibilities can be.

Job descriptions differ from information contained in an employee handbook because a handbook outlines policies and procedures that apply to all employees, such as no drugs or cigarettes; no refund without receipt; no covering shifts without manager's written approval; and so on. Policies are the don'ts of an organization, whereas procedures are the how to do things, the step-by-step ways to clock in on your register, for example, or request a day off. These have no place in a job description but are extremely valuable parts of an employee handbook.

Know Who You Want as an Employee

One of the first steps doctors take when patients are suffering from health problems is to look at their diets. In some cases, they require that patients record all of their meals in a food journal to know exactly what they're putting into their bodies. They want their patients to realize that their *own* choices are what might be making them sick. Similarly, business owners' problems often can be traced back to the hiring process; who they've allowed to represent their brand to the world is akin to the foods that we put in our bodies. Both have a profound effect.

If you're approached at the start of your busy season by an employee who sheepishly says to you, "I'm giving notice," you immediately panic. Much like a person on a diet faced with stress, you want to do *something*—right at that moment. And much like a dieter may give in and grab the chocolate cake, you probably leave your office and run to hang a Help Wanted sign in your window. You're so grateful that *anyone* comes in, that—often without

SAMPLE MANAGER JOB DESCRIPTION

Job Specifications:

Previous experience as a management trainee or assistant manager. Must be able to manage, supervise, read, and understand job related documents and perform simple arithmetic calculations.

Duties and Responsibilities:

1. Motivate subordinates to sell and ensure that store achieves sales goals each month.
2. Recruit job applicants. Screen, interview, and hire competent candidates.
3. Supervise and train all store personnel, including shift managers and hourly employees.
4. Must have complete working knowledge of, must comply with, and must administer and implement all policies and procedures in the handbook to ensure proper and lawful administration of policies.
5. Must demonstrate thorough working knowledge of products.
6. Must act in a professional and reliable manner to set an example for subordinate employees.
7. Responsible for knowing when scheduled to work and then reporting promptly in uniform 5 minutes before each shift. Responsible for reading all handouts, sales boosters, shift log, product knowledge materials and owner communications.
8. Schedule subordinates to ensure proper staff coverage.
9. Oversee store operations to ensure store is opened promptly each day and has sufficient coverage.
10. Plan, direct, and delegate work assignments to subordinates.
11. Assist subordinates as needed. Demonstrate courteous communications skills to customers and other employees.
12. Evaluate employees' efficiency, productivity, and overall performance. Recommend advancement, pay increases for, promotions and other status changes of subordinates.
13. Oversee the maintenance of the appearance and security of both the facility and products.
14. Provide for safety of employees and company property and conduct safety training meetings.
15. Handle employee grievances and customer complaints.
16. Control flow and distribution of materials and supplies.
17. Order, monitor and control store inventory levels and product quantities.
18. Monitor for theft and enforce strict cash control policies.
19. Perform daily banking functions.
20. Other responsibilities as may be delegated by the company from time to time.

IMMEDIATE SUPERVISOR: Owner, Regional Supervisor

I HAVE READ, UNDERSTAND AND WILL FULFILL THE JOB SPECIFICATIONS, DUTIES AND RESPONSIBILITIES OUTLINED ABOVE. IF I BECOME AWARE OF A VIOLATION OF POLICY OR PROCEDURE, I WILL BRING THE MATTER TO THE ATTENTION OF THE OWNER.

_____

Employee Signature   Date

_____

Manager Signature   Date

FIGURE 3.1   A Sample Manager's Job Description

Source: Copyright © 2010 Bob Phibbs, www.retaildoc.com.

considering whether this is truly the *best* person for the organization—you settle. Over time, because you haven't given much thought with each hire, you may have built a team that cannot deliver the results. You have the water boys from the baseball team, when what you need are the A-Rods.

You can fix this and grow your business in a positive direction by knowing exactly what you want in a great employee—as well as what you *don't*. And by the way, friendliness is a given. So review your job descriptions and decide which qualities are most important to you.

Employee Attributes to Value
- ◆ Beating sales goals
- ◆ Being on time
- ◆ Executing exceptional customer service
- ◆ Managing a winning team
- ◆ Taking initiative
- ◆ Playing well with others
- ◆ Training in your field
- ◆ Exhibiting attention to detail
- ◆ Taking personal responsibility
- ◆ Being familiar with your neighborhood
- ◆ Having knowledge of your competitors

Applicants to Avoid
- ◆ People who can't get to work on time
- ◆ People more comfortable doing nothing
- ◆ Constant complainers
- ◆ People who operate at a minimum
- ◆ Underachievers
- ◆ Blamers

Your list helps you to prepare questions that will get the answers you need from your applicants. It will also become a lot easier to make hiring choices once you identify which qualities are most important to you.

How to Create Your Interview Questions

Imagine a romantic first date. You're at the perfect spot, at the perfect time of day, and your date just keeps asking questions. "So where did you go to school?" "What do you like to do in your off time?" "What attracted you to my profile?" It would seem awkward to receive questions that are so direct and one-sided, yes? Yet this is precisely what most people do when they conduct interviews. They don't know what they want, but ask a bunch of questions because someone told them to just ask open-ended questions during interviews.

We're going to change that.

I want you to understand *what* you are looking for before you ask any questions. For example: What are your best employee's top five characteristics? What five questions could you ask potential employees to see if they share those characteristics? What are the three grades you could give them for each—with an "A" meaning that they've exceeded expectations, "C" for average, and "F" being a deal killer?

Past behavior predicts future successes, so don't ask hypothetical questions like, "What would you do if . . . " or "How would you handle . . . " These are merely interview placeholders. Managers and owners often don't give much thought to what the best answer would look like in situations like these; therefore, they craft questions that are worthless. You know, questions like "Can you tell me a little bit about yourself?" or "What would you do if a customer came in for a refund without a receipt?" or "Where do you see yourself in five years with us?"

The answers to these questions don't tell you anything of real value. They just take up your valuable time. All of them are crap. Why? Repeat each of them out loud. What is the A answer for each one? Can you even tell? How would they—or *you*—truly even know what they would do until they'd been trained to your standards? If you don't know—*don't ask.* Only ask questions about applicants' experience at another job or event to judge how they handle themselves.

Since you are looking for someone who can sell, make sure to include a couple of questions that help you assess their comfort level and thoughts about selling. For example, "We don't just clerk the merchandise to our customers; we sell it. Can you describe one of the biggest sales you made and how it demonstrated your abilities?"

To find out if they have the needed drive, ask something like: "No one makes 100 percent of sales. What goes through your head when you lose a sale?" To get a feel for their self-motivation, ask, "What was the most memorable bonus, commission, or achievement you made as a result of exceeding a sales goal?"

One oft-used, shopworn question is to ask an interviewee: "Can you sell me this pen?" The problem is that this really only shows if he or she can point out features; not whether the person can actually sell. Doing this assumes that the customer trusts you and has both the desire and time to process the reasons to purchase the applicant spouts.

The sweet spot, where you want to get the customer, is to have him trust you enough to lower his defenses and tell you honestly *why* he wants to change from the pen he's been using to your product, and what he hopes it will accomplish. When a salesperson begins "pitching" a product without understanding these reasons, it can lead to assumptions that derail the sale. Hiring them because they can fumble through this exercise is not a good way to grow profits. In the next chapter we talk extensively about how to build trust, but for now, avoid the pen question.

Here are six statements and questions designed to determine how well an applicant has exhibited the qualities you're seeking as well as some ways to spot the behaviors that you want to avoid:

1. *"Please describe a typical day at your last job from clock in to clock out."* You'll want to listen for skills and abilities—like being detail-oriented or a self-starter—that might transfer to the position you are hiring for.

2. *"Please give me five reasons why I should hire you."* You're looking for a candidate's ability to sell herself; "I need a job" does not qualify as a reason. If she can't come up with five positive things about herself—something about which she knows *everything*—how will she ever sell your $1,000 window treatment, barbeque tools, or tax preparation service?

3. *"Please describe a specific time when you went out of your way for a customer and why."* This will help you uncover how hospitable and empathetic the applicant is, and it will give you the chance to hear about a specific customer interaction.

4. *"Can you describe a specific time when you had a problem with a customer and tell me how you handled it?"* This shows you how well the individual is able to deal with conflict when handling customer demands. It also can give you clues to his personality type based on his response.

5. *"Can you give me a specific time when you had a problem with a coworker and how you resolved it?"* This will help you understand the candidate's interpersonal skills and how well the individual relates to colleagues.

6. Tell your candidate: *"This position requires you to work a schedule that includes mornings and weekends. Are there any reasons that you would be unable to fulfill those requirements?"* You want to find out as early as possible whether the applicant has a vacation coming up in two months, will be moving, or has to work another job every third and fourth Saturday.

How long should an interview take? No more than 20 minutes. Yes, Amiables—*that's it.* You only have a 51 percent chance of making a good hire—that's the equivalent of a coin toss—and spending more time on the interview will not improve those odds. You won't know if an individual is truly a good fit until you see her in training.

You want to connect with your interviewee as a person first, so begin by asking about the weather or a Window of Contact (from Chapter 4) to start the dialogue. Your goal is to have pleasant chitchat for a minute or two—like you would with a friend—rather than immediately assuming the role of judging interviewer. Louise Montgomery, co-owner of It's A Grind Coffee House, began by asking every job applicant if she could get them a coffee drink or pastry before the interview. This set the welcoming tone for how she expected employees to treat visitors to their coffeehouses.

As your interviewee talks, try to discern if he is a Thinker or a Feeler and then which of the four types of personalities he most clearly exhibits. No one is exclusively one type, but with practice, you should be able to identify which your candidate most closely approximates fairly quickly. Expressives tend to be the easiest to identify because you can tell by their clothes, tattoos, or color choices of accessories. Drivers are all about themselves and their awards; Analyticals just care about the facts; and Amiables are all about what you do and your business. The better you get at deciphering these differences, the easier it is to train, coach, motivate, reprimand, and promote your employees, because you understand how each one looks at the world.

Jobs Where Each of the Four Personalities Commonly Are Found

Over the years I've observed how the four personalities naturally are attracted to certain positions. Drivers are the commissioned salespeople with quotas to meet and awards that rank their abilities. Expressives are often opening crews of new stores because they love the thrill of everything being new. Analyticals are typically seen with computers and other electronics where their technical prowess is most valued. Amiables can be seen frequently in fast food because the experience of being with friends on a crew is stronger than selling the products.

Review the candidate's name on the application; does he prefer to be called what's printed or a nickname? (For example: Bob instead of Robert.) Write the candidate's preference above his name. Read off the phone number, then circle it. You don't want to go to call the individual and find you can't distinguish his 7s from his 9s. Ask no more than 10 questions from your list. Then talk about your business: when you started, what you do, services you offer, training you provide, and so on. This is especially important to the Feeler personalities. What makes you an excellent employer? Don't lose sight of the fact that job candidates are interviewing you to determine what sort of place your company is to work at as well. Show them a trainee job description; explain pay scale, training, and any uniform requirements. These things are especially important to Thinker personalities.

Preparing for Their Answers: Best, Average, Failing

While I was training 20 new franchisees owners, I came to the section where I explained how to hire a great team. The participants were to come up with one question they felt would best help them determine whether they would hire an applicant. After they all had their one question, we got into a semicircle and they each shared theirs. The group interviewed four applicants, and each franchisee asked him or her one question. Things were going well until the interviewees got to Gary and he asked with a straight face, "Why are manhole covers round?" The applicants looked to me, to the rest of the group, up in the air, down at their feet, out the window—anything to avoid the question. After an awkward silence or giggle, they would try their best: "Because they are?" "I don't know." "So the alligators can't get out?" No one knew what was expected from the interchange. We were all somewhat stunned, however, we continued the exercise without commenting.

Once we were done, we asked the applicants to evaluate each of the questions. All four said the same thing of Gary's question: "I didn't know how to answer that." Gary tried to defend his question by saying, "I always like to mix things up and catch my interviewees off guard to see how they handle pressure."

An interesting take, to be sure, but you're not looking to trip up a good employee and make them feel stupid, are you? Don't you want the best and brightest to feel comfortable with you from the start? And what *was* a potential A response to that odd question? Even Gary himself didn't know.

The point here is to seriously consider what qualities a great applicant should possess; create questions that will help them shine by spotlighting past behavior; and know what an A, C, or F answer is before you ever ask the question. For example, if tardiness is an issue for you, you might want to ask: "Can you tell me about a time when you were late for a shift and how you dealt with it?" The A answer here is: "I'm never tardy. I always believe in being ready to clock in five minutes early. The C answer might be, "I called in and told them before my shift was to begin to see if someone could cover for me." The F answer is, "I've got a pretty cool manager and he lets me clock in whenever I get there."

Responsibility is an important quality to pin down during an interview. I had one applicant who, when asked about past behaviors, said, "I was working with a guy who was on the phone the whole night. We had a lot of work to do, and he just stayed on the phone. It was getting to be about a half hour before we were to lock up; and I went over to him while he was on the phone and said, 'Dude, I need help so we can get this place clean and we can go home.' He did, and we got along from then on." That was the A answer. He didn't say he ignored his coworker and whined later to his manager, which would have been an F response.

An A answer to your question, "Can you describe one of the biggest sales you made, and how it demonstrated your abilities?" would describe the circumstances, how the customer came in for one inexpensive item, walked out with much more and came back after telling her friends. An A answer to, "What goes through your head when you lose a sale?" would express how the potential employee felt bad, and how he, the customer, and the store lost out. He might also describe his process for replaying the sale to find what he could do better.

But before we get to the actual interview—where do we go to find good potential employees?

Recruiting

You've decided what qualities you're looking for in a new employee, what your interview questions will be, and what an A answer will sound like. Now—how are you going to attract job candidates? There are several ways to approach this depending on who you're looking for.

Use your signage to spread the word that you're looking for fun and interesting people. Figures 3.2, 3.3, and 3.4 that follow show some examples of ones I've posted in the window.

FIGURE **3.2** Be Different in a Good Way with Your Hiring Signs

There are real superstars out there in restaurants, dry cleaners, and the mall, yet many times we passively wait for the good ones to come to us. The very best way to recruit employees is to see them in action, so carry your business cards when you are out shopping or dining. Then, when you find a great potential employee, you can hand it to the

FIGURE **3.3** Show You Have a Sense of Humor

BECAUSE YOUR
BOYFRIEND
WILL EVENTUALLY
ASK FOR
GAS MONEY
NOW HIRING
APPLY IN PERSON WITH MANAGER

FIGURE 3.4   This Can Attract Expressives, the Spark Plug to Your Crew

person and casually say, "I think you're great; if you're looking for more hours, please contact me." Here are a few others you may not have considered but could harness the power of social media:

◆ Update your Facebook status to alert others to the fact that you're looking for additional employees or adding shifts.

◆ Take out a location-based paid Facebook ad that targets your zip code.

◆ Create a video post on YouTube or your own web site featuring your employees, what a typical day might be like, and who an ideal candidate would be. You can also post this to your Facebook fan page or include it in an e-mail blast to your list. Put a positive spin on it by saying you're "adding shifts," and then list them; this keeps someone you're thinking of getting rid of from figuring it out.

◆ You can still post your job with the local college or university online job board and get results. This works well because college students are much more likely than high school teenagers, who live at home with Mom and Dad, to need the job and the money.

Not Much Help

Some ideas sound good initially, but don't turn out to be very useful or fruitful in practice. For example:

◆ You might consider asking your employees if they have any friends who are looking for extra hours. While this sounds good in theory, the best potential employees usually have jobs already. Those Feelers who don't often will apply so they can talk to their friend at work.

◆ You can ask customers about prospective hires, but they'll often recommend their son or daughter, which can make it tricky when it comes time to reprimand or fire. Trust me on this.

◆ Post an ad on Monster.com, Yahoo!, Craigslist, or HR.com. You often get lost in the millions of job postings and might receive a barrage of automatic e-mails from people who have no interest or abilities to work for you.

◆ You can take out an ad in a community newspaper's want ads, but mostly high school kids are looking there, which means limited availability and many times lack of responsibility.

How to Review Your Applications

So now that you've got a pile of applications—what next? Here are nine points to consider:

1. Is all the information filled out? If you want a very detail-oriented person, probably an Analytical, missing information signals that the applicant is not the one for the job.
2. Did the candidate include the name of her supervisor with phone number as well as area code? You don't have time to be running around trying to look up the contact information for example of Bob's Bofo Pizza in Poughkeepsie, New York.

3. Is his handwriting legible? Sloppy handwriting might indicate that this is not his ideal job, or that he's in too much of a hurry to get something done to complete the task with care.

4. Are there gaps in employment? Eight months off between jobs might indicate that the candidate worked for someone else from whom she's worried she won't get a good recommendation.

5. How long did the prospect stay at his previous jobs? It's rare to find people who work for one employer for years; however, when every previous job only lasts a few months, that individual never really became a part of a profitable business. We see this particularly with people who work in malls.

6. How close does the candidate live to your business? On one level, it can be great for someone to live down the block; on the other, it might mean that friends and family are likely to drop by throughout the day and distract your new employee.

7. Can the candidate work the hours required? Print them at the top of the application. Think in terms of your scheduling. For example, someone who claims to be able to work from "6 to closing" won't be much help if your last shift starts at 4. You have to hire to the schedule, not schedule to the employees. Otherwise it will take you three to four hours to create your schedule each week.

8. Why does the person claim to have left her last job? "Personal reasons" could be another way to try to hide the fact that she was fired or left under a cloud of suspicion. Remember: past behavior determines future success with your business.

9. Be aware of the siren's call of "previous experience" because an applicant worked for a competitor. Though it's tempting to assume that you won't have to train the person on the products, you may end up hearing, "We did it this way," over and over. Can the prospect be open to your ideas of customer service and training? If you ask him this, he will, of course, claim that he can, so listen to the pronouns of "they" versus "we." "They" usually means the applicant can let go of his previous

employer, while "we" may mean he was too attached. A franchisee I worked with found this out when her employee kept comparing our brand to Starbucks. One day the franchisee had enough and said, "Why do you keep saying that? You're here now." The manager answered, "Come on, we all know they are better." The manager was gone that instant, but only after the owner had invested a month in trying to train her. The old saying that "It is hard to change the spots on a leopard" holds true.

Don't let a statement of "no previous experience" stop you from considering an applicant. If the potential employee is personable and makes a good first impression, find other information to use during your interview. Ask for examples from their club, hobby, or team to get the necessary A answers. I have often found upbeat, positive people with no experience to be some of the best salespeople, because they have no preconceived notions about what it means to wait on customers. In fact, Dave Wetzel, Senior Director of Franchise Development and Operations at The Coffee Bean & Tea Leaf, told me that one of the best employees he ever hired had no previous experience. Dave asked more questions about hobbies and found the applicant raised prize-winning rabbits. He heard about specific instances during which the applicant had exhibited attention to detail, was on time, and had a winning spirit by adapting his questions to the individual in front of him.

While these nine factors are not deal killers in and of themselves, if there are too many warning signs that exist together, you might want to put the particular applicant in a "maybe" pile to save your time.

Setting the Stage for the Interview

The odds of a good hire are only about 50/50 for many reasons. While you might find the best person for the job is a Driver, you might end up partnering him with an Expressive manager who found him to be a threat and sabotaged him. Maybe your company doesn't have a good training program for that personality, or perhaps she simply wasn't trainable. Maybe the job doesn't have enough stimulation for the sharp ones or too much for the dull to keep up. These are all reasons why it is important to view hiring solely as an employee's entry into the game—not a win. Likewise, remember that hiring is the start of a process for you—not the conclusion. Your goal is to find friendly people who are interested in meeting other people. That means that you ask yourself from the moment you meet them, "Do they have a welcoming attitude?" We're looking for people to greet customers with their arms wide open, not crossed across their chest hiding behind the counter.

Begin by arranging a time that is convenient for you; just before lunch or midafternoon often works well. Hold interviews in your back office or a corner of a local coffeehouse where you won't be distracted by the needs of your crew, customers, or phone calls. Stay out of the food court of the mall or on a bench in front of your store if you want Feelers to relax and focus on your interview. Make sure you have some Post-it notes so that you can make notes to jog your memory when you're sifting through applications (they can be removed once the applicant has either passed that process or not.)

Feelers, keep in mind that you're interviewing a potential new employee, not a potential new mate from Match.com. You only need 20 minutes to determine if this person is a good fit or not. Take time here Thinkers, Feeler personalities will need time to become comfortable, so if necessary, force yourself to use at least 15 minutes for each. Schedule all the interviews accordingly with a break for yourself preplanned.

Who you hire will ultimately determine how well your business does, so the owner or manager should be involved from the beginning. Accept the fact that you won't truly know how good recent hires will be until they are being trained. The goal of your interview is to make it a *reasonable* roll of the dice, not a wild card.

Oh, and one more thing: You will never be able to change the culture of your business if you hire by consensus or according to who your existing crew likes. Many times they could be threatened by a self-assured Driver or energetic Expressive.

Deal Killers

Reasons to Pass on an Applicant

I was preparing to visit an It's A Grind franchise that was opening in southern California. Though the franchisee had previously managed a couple of convenience stores, the coffee business was new to him. The "go live" trainers had said they were concerned about the type of people on the crew and wanted some feedback. I walked in the door to find three employees standing behind the counter, not saying a word. A fourth employee was playing his guitar in the corner, while another walked past me silently.

I met with the crew at the owner's request to "get them pumped up." I explained how our concept was different from our competitors, how we wanted to create exceptional experiences for everyone we met, and finished with some pointers on how to engage customers.

The guy playing guitar when I came in? Left the meeting and never came back. The rest were just as lifeless afterward as when I walked in. I sat down with the owner to share my concerns about this not being a good crew to open with. They had no personality, either as a group or individually. They seemed like drones. He replied, "I didn't hire them for personality. Coming from Circle K, I just wanted to make sure they didn't steal from me." Okay then—that spoke volumes! The owner hadn't changed his (somewhat desperate) hiring profile from the last store he managed. He hadn't considered who would make the best employee for a coffeehouse. We therefore agreed to hold off opening until he could find and hire the right kind of staff members.

Being afraid to approach and speak to customers aren't the only qualities that can be considered deal killers. Don't waste your time with potential employees if they are:

◆ Not friendly.
◆ Mumbling.
◆ Unable to communicate at the level the job requires.
◆ Unable to take responsibility for their previous actions.
◆ Unable to draw attention to themselves and sell you on hiring them over someone else.

Another sticking point is being late to an interview. A restaurant owner friend of mine named Christian related a story in which he had completed a 10-minute interview with a prospective new waiter. The guy was a perfect fit, and Christian finished by saying, "I would really like to have hired you, but you were late for the interview." The applicant's expression turned from elation to confusion. "But I hit traffic."

"I see you have a cell phone. I gave you my cell number and said to let me know if you couldn't make it. Do you remember?"

"Yes, but that was if I couldn't make it."

"I can't hire someone who doesn't think of my business first. That could have been a shift where someone ready to leave was expecting you to arrive. I would have been running one person down for 20 minutes. I'm letting you know this for your next interview."

An applicant should show you his best side from the moment you meet. Therefore, if it doesn't go well during the interview—if the applicant is giving single word answers with eyes flitting around the room, or if she keeps asking you to repeat yourself because she doesn't understand—don't continue the interview. Cut it short and cut your losses. A client of mine recently had an applicant who received a text message during the interview and instead of letting it go, asked, "Mind if I get that?"

The goal is to hire someone who will do a great job when on your payroll, so any contact you have with an individual prior to saying, "You're hired," should reflect her best self.

Don't Fall in Love   Hiring choices directly affect how much product you move, how your team works together, and what your daily stress level might be. We're frequently so relieved to find someone that we only hear the good in any response—like a lonely person on a blind date. We tell ourselves the applicant is great, or at least not so bad and *then* look for reasons to affirm it. This is somewhat akin to walking into a bar at closing time, finding the worst possible person for you, and marrying him.

So if all the answers you hear sound great, and you want to hire that person right then and there: *Stop yourself.* You need to obtain at least one more piece of information in order to get a balanced view of this applicant and that comes from seeking opposite information.

If you don't find the bad with the good, you convince yourself this is a great hire instead of deciding whether it's the right fit. Balance is the key; you want to know an employee's strengths and weaknesses before she begins, not on your dime. If your interviewee told you that he did so well with customer service at his past job that a customer wrote a letter recommending his work, you need to balance that with a time he didn't do such a great job. Look for opposite information by asking, "Can you tell me about an instance during which you did *not* give great customer service—and how you handled that?" Some applicants—particularly Drivers—will immediately say, "I never had bad experiences." That's when you have to stay with that question and not let them off the hook. They're testing your ability as a manager, so keep digging for information.

Your next line could be something like, "I'm sure we can agree that none of us is perfect, right?" Wait for him to agree with a nod or "Yes." Continue, "Good. So there must have been at least one time you can think of. See it clearly in your mind, how you might have not done the best job with a customer and the end result. It's okay to take a minute to come up with the answer." Then literally bite your tongue if need be, but don't say anything until he does.

What is the good, better, and best answer to that question? An A answer would be, "When I used to work at a Denny's restaurant, I had a customer who was really upset that his food was cold. I put the ticket in late and got busy, and I didn't realize that it had been waiting there for so long. He got angry and called me names. I apologized, told him that his dinner was on me, and told the manager afterward." Maybe a C response for you would be, "I apologized to the customer, took the meal back, had it remade, and asked if there was anything else I could do." A failing answer would be, "I told my manager, and he handled it." Remember that the way they've behaved previously will predict their future behavior. Do you want to have everyone's problems dumped on you to correct? Of course not.

If a candidate said he was always on time, ask him to describe one time that he wasn't and how he handled it. If she was an Analytical who said she took great pains to know every product's features, ask her to remember a time she didn't know the answers to a customer's questions and how she handled it. You can use that same hunt for contrary information about a time a candidate had trouble with another employee or for how he reacted to a policy with which he disagreed but had to follow.

Listen to your interviewees' answers as though you're casting for a movie. Too often, we hire the exact same personality over and over again, which gives your business a one-dimensional view. You might like Julia Roberts, but you wouldn't want to watch a movie where she played all the parts. All right, maybe some of you would, but the point is you need as varied a crew as possible. You should strive to include all four personalities on your sales team.

How Will Your Applicants Personality Push Your Buttons?

Drivers can react negatively to other Driver personalities by feeling threatened that someone else can shine and not them. Drivers can react negatively to Analytical personalities because they are too quiet; their lengthy explanations of "how to build a watch" instead of give the time can frustrate. Drivers can react negatively to Expressives, who can seem phony due to all their zeal. Drivers can react negatively to Amiables, who want too much personal information.

Analyticals can react negatively to other Analyticals because the other person may know more than him or her. Analyticals can react negatively to Drivers because of their desire to win, skip details, or bluntly ask about benefits. Analyticals can react negatively to Expressives because their unfocused energy can rattle the Analytical's sense of order. Analyticals can react negatively to Amiables because they talk too much, rather than focusing on the question at hand.

Expressives can react negatively to other Expressives because the other person isn't noticing them as the boss. Expressives can react negatively to the Driver because of their push for sales, rather than having fun. Expressives can react negatively to Analyticals because of their need for detail. Expressives can react negatively to the other Feeler, the Amiable, because of their lack of speaking up.

Amiables can react negatively to other Amiables because they don't know how to motivate them—they just want to be liked. Amiables can react negatively with Drivers because Drivers need to compete and win—the opposite of the Amiables wanting to just help. Amiables can react negatively to Analyticals because they are often more reserved and less likely to come out and share about their personal lives. Amiables can react negatively to Expressives because all they want to do is "have fun."

In short, all of us have buttons the other personalities can push but if we are to grow, we need to continuously look at our reaction to the other person for clues on how to minimize these built-in possibilities for conflict.

Balance the Four Personality Types A smart manager finds that the personalities who hate to do what you love to do are the personalities who love to do what you hate—and hires accordingly to fill those gaps. A good goal when hiring is to balance your sales force between the four types, because too many of any type will have dire consequences. Too many Analyticals, and everything is nit-picked. All Amiables won't sell anything, everyone's just chatting. A team full of Drivers—especially on a commission sales force—will constantly provoke fights over whose sale is whose. Too many Expressives and no one will show up to open the store on a beautiful day—they'll all be surfing with their buds.

But each type of personality has its strengths as well. For instance, an Analytical will show up for work during a snowstorm because it's "the right thing to do." While they can be good at retail, they are going to concentrate on keeping the store clean and stocked—due to their logical mind-set—when there is no structure or direction. And if they get bored with that, they'll sit on their haunches and wait. The challenge with all Thinkers on a crew is that you don't generally have the warmth of the Feelers to make your store more caring and fun.

On the other hand, Expressives are drawn to new stores. They love the excitement and thrive on the chaos, which can wear off as the store settles into routine, and then they look elsewhere for excitement. An Amiable will get a job to meet people and make friends—either behind the counter or in the aisles. She might get flustered at the register but be really good at interacting with customers. You might have a compromise to make in this situation; if she is great at back and forth with customers, can you afford to have her deal solely with them, requiring someone else to ring them up?

Finishing the Interview   If you are impressed with a particular interviewee, tell him exactly what makes you such a great boss and what your job training entails. If, for example, you spot tattoos on him and have a dress code prohibiting visible tattoos, ask now if he would be willing to cover them while at work. If not, then pass. Have all applicants read over your job description to see if they have any questions or problems signing it. When you have done all of that ask, "Do you have any questions for me that I haven't answered regarding the job?" If you plan to hire someone without a second interview, give her your business card and have her call back the next day at 4 P.M., after you've had a chance to check references. (This is one more way to see if someone really wants to work for you.) If you don't think you'll hire someone, tell him you'll be reviewing applications all week and hope to call people back next week. Drivers, if you feel bold, tell the candidate right then that you don't think it's a fit.

Some business owners like to have a second interview because they want to see the applicant at another time of day. However, applicants can get the impression that your granting a second interview means that the job is theirs. I only recommend one interview for an entry-level position because again, the odds of a good hire are about the same as a coin toss. Don't worry, Feelers, if you've followed these guidelines, you should be well on your way to improving your team.

When the applicant returns your call at 4 P.M. the next day, tell her what time to show up, what to wear, what to bring (Social Security card and driver's license, or other form of ID) and tell her with whom she'll be training. Also, let her know that she cannot work for you if she does not bring those items; you don't have time to chase after a new hire to comply with federal regulations.

The Retail Doc's Secret Weapon for Checking References

There was no question about calling for references in the old days—you'd just do it. Nowadays, between being too busy and in too much of a hurry to fill the slot and labor laws that have made former employers skittish about telling the truth, owners have largely abandoned the process. This is dangerous; you could easily be hiring someone who's just been fired from a previous job. So here's my secret weapon to get that information: the weather.

When calling on a work reference, always introduce yourself, give your title and company. Ask the appropriate person if the applicant is eligible for rehire. If you hit a roadblock, "We don't give out that information. We only verify dates of employment and rate of pay," switch to the weather. Say, "I'm sure when you hired him it was a bright, sunny day; can you tell me the weather when he left?" Usually the person will tell you with a chuckle, "Oh, it was very sunny," which means things were good, or, as one gentleman told me, "Rainy, stormy—a hurricane."

You can get the information you're looking for; you just have to pick up the phone and ask for it in the right way. Another way to check references is to enter an applicant's name on Google. Sometimes a Facebook, MySpace, YouTube, or blog post will appear and you can see how the person interacts with friends, or occasionally, rail against his or her employer.

Deciding Who to Hire

Before you say, "You're hired!" to an applicant the next day, consider what could happen if you had to get rid of him or her. One Expressive business owner—Gary, from the manhole question earlier—hired an 83-year-old grandmother because, as he claimed, "I liked her attitude." While it's a good idea to hire for attitude and train the skills, she couldn't cut it a month later, and Gary was stuck because he simply wasn't able to face the thought of firing her. Who could feel good about crushing the expectations of such a kind, elderly woman? No one.

One more thing to remember about hiring is to hire the hungry, not the starving. Someone who needs a job—*any job*—so badly that he tells you that during the interview might be indicating that he doesn't necessarily want to work for you. Even if the candidate passes the interview with flying colors, she may end up departing within a month when another offer comes in or leaving your store with product under her coat. Keep this at the top of your mind when speaking to potential staff members.

> ### *STAT: Five Things to Do Immediately after Reading This Chapter*
>
> 1. Review the last interview you did. How many questions did you ask based on applicants' past experiences? How many were hypotheticals?
> 2. Write out your 10 questions to ask everyone.
> 3. Review your hiring criteria. What A-caliber answers are you looking for?
> 4. Write down what type of personalities you have on your crew now and what roles you need to fill: the Analytical, detail-obsessed person; the Expressive spark plug; and so on.
> 5. Role-play your new interview questions with a friend to make sure you are comfortable with the new process.

Chapter 4

Sell It or You're Dead

Much like your lungs have to pull oxygen into them or the entire organism dies, your employees have to be able to direct customers to merchandise and help them see that the product matches or exceeds their need—or your business is dead. This chapter will show you the step-by-step sales process that builds on your good hiring skills and brings in the big bucks. The goal is to create an exceptional experience for everyone you meet—something that comes about most reliably when you use the procedure I've designed to double sales in thousands of businesses worldwide. I call it the "Five Parts to a Successful Sale" (see Figure 4.1 on page 79).

The Greeting

♦ We greet people like they are coming to our home in a friendly and positive manner by using words that most of our competitors never use.

♦ We welcome customers within 15 seconds to make store visitors feel comfortable (and reduce theft).

♦ We use a prop (like a sample, a book, or other product) to deflect any anxiety that either the employee or customer may have about initially greeting the other.

♦ Customers are more likely to respond favorably if our own attitude is favorable.

♦ We let customers browse a bit and then return to make a positive statement about something they are looking at.

◆ Store tours help to show everything that we offer quickly and concisely to new customers.

Windows of Contact

◆ Before we begin to "pitch" the customer, we need to make a personal connection and build trust using the formula compliment, share, and continue.

◆ We need to recognize the person in front of us as unique and share something about ourselves that cements a memorable impression in the customer's mind.

Your Question

◆ We ask one general question that cannot be answered with a "yes" or "no" to help narrow the customer's choices.

Features and Benefits

◆ We point out a specific feature of a product (the facts), and what benefit it delivers to the customer. This helps whittle many choices down to a manageable two or three.

Closing with an Add-on

◆ We paint a picture of one additional item so well that the customer allows himself to splurge. This is often called upselling, and it is one of the most effective ways to drive average transaction as well as profitability.

◆ We suggest only *one* complementary item, not a laundry list.

When a client's high-end dealers put this process in place, their sales jumped over 20 percent within *four months*. I'll show you why this selling system is so effective, give some examples to use in training, and illustrate exactly how you can customize it to your own business. Once you develop a culture of sales—not "so what"—when customers look at your merchandise, you'll find that it's easy to maintain.

FIGURE **4.1**   Five Parts to a Successful Sale

Touch Every Personality to Get the Sale

As customers, the four personalities have some very similar and dissimilar aspects. Each has needs that have to be addressed in a fashion they can understand. That can only happen when you have a selling system. Why do you need such a system? Because of the conflicts that arise when the four personalities only sell according to their natural style:

- ◆ Drivers tend to jump from A ahead to F and expect others to fill in B, D, and E and catch up on their own. Because of this, Drivers often lose Analyticals because those leaps or gaps stick in Analyticals' minds. Analyticals can't proceed until the Driver goes back and the Analytical can hear every detail explained, since they need to move logically from A to B to C. Drivers can become very upset at Analyticals' "stickler" responses that make them explain every detail. Feelers in the presence of Drivers can get a sense of being steamrolled or "sold" rather than feeling as though they made a decision to buy, since the Driver might be trying to hurry up the process or pushing a premium product that the Driver likes.

◆ Analyticals who give every detail to anyone other than an Analytical might end up hearing a lot of "Just looking" in response; Feeler personalities are burdened by the kind of technical jargon that flips the "I'm an idiot" switch. Feelers will try to politely pull themselves away and run. Drivers who have to deal with an Analytical salesperson will often just interrupt the Analytical's spewing of features and technical jargon and ask about something else if they don't hear quickly enough about how a product will meet *their* needs. Analyticals also tend to want to "tie down" customers by finding out exactly how much they want to spend so they don't waste their time looking at too much. This limits their effectiveness with anyone but mission shoppers or other Analyticals. The Analytical comes from the logical mind-set that says, "They'll ask if they want anything." They also tend to overload customers with product features, which is the opposite of Expressives, who tend to naturally present everything in a matter-of-fact way.

◆ Expressives will show all four personalities lots of possibilities. While this creativity is what makes them so great at designing, music, and sales, they can easily lose the Thinkers because they present too many possibilities that are not the main product the Thinker is seeking. This makes the task of choosing frustrating for Thinkers as well as overwhelming for Amiables. In fact, Expressives and Analyticals can overwhelm customers with so much information that they can't decide what is and isn't important; the Analytical favors the technical stuff, while the Expressives focus on the creative stuff. Expressives will tend to talk about the benefits of a product rather than the features (like an Analytical). Amiables want Expressives' myriad of choices narrowed down, and more often than not, they like having one option selected for them over all others. The Expressives' natural inclination to show multiple possibilities might require customers to bring them back to the product they are considering right now instead of *all* the possibilities. Expressives might push a product because they think it's "cool"—not because it will do everything that the customer needs. Their natural enthusiasm can also inflate products' benefits without devoting time to adequately explaining why because Expressives may jump the gun and try to fix something without all the information.

♦ Amiables often get overly personal and ask a lot of questions that can frustrate Thinkers. Amiables' natural aversion to saying the wrong thing can make closing the sale much more difficult for them *and* the customer. Amiables are patient to a fault so they will empathize with customers who are "just looking," or have to "think about it." Amiables ask a lot of questions because they want to get to know the person, and the notion of selling something to the individual may never cross their minds if they feel they are connecting to another person in a meaningful way.

Figure 4.1, which depicts The Five Parts to a Successful Sale, shows how each of the four personalities needs to be addressed.

Opposites

♦ Drivers and Amiables
♦ Expressives and Analyticals

Clerking versus Selling

I was having lunch one day with Gordon Segal, the founder of Crate & Barrel, and talking about why so many stores are struggling. I maintained it was because they got too comfy not having to sell the merch. Gordon added, "You know, you're right, back in the '60s and '70s we *had* to sell."

Many business owners nowadays call their employees *salespeople* when all they're really doing is picking the low hanging fruit. Here's how "low-hanging-fruit" clerking goes:

Customer walks in. Employee yells across the counter, "How are you today? Looking for anything special?"

Customer replies, "No," and looks around alone. After awhile, he asks the employee, "Do you have this widget?"

"I do, right over here."

"I'll take it."

That is not selling.

That is about as much like selling as a guy walking into a Ford dealership and saying to the salesperson, "I'm looking for the Mustang GT five-speed in grey with black seats," and the salesman responding, "Right over here."

That is *clerking*, and it is what too often passes for "customer service." A *real* sale would be if the guy came in for a Ford Focus and drove off in the Mustang because the salesperson asked questions and established a relationship, and the customer opened up and admitted that he had wanted one ever since he was a teenager in Toledo, Ohio, and first saw it on the *Ed Sullivan Show.*

True selling is going after the whole tree, not just picking what you can reach without effort. *Selling* makes the difference, for example, when the wife says, "you better think about it," or when the customer selects a product that won't do what he wants it to do. It's not our job to prejudge what customers can afford, but we can safely assume if they're standing there that they're interested in purchasing. It's not pushy; it's one of the most profitable ways to grow your business.

When I was selling western wear in college, I had a guy who came into the store and told me that he needed a red shirt for a party. "Why red?" I asked. "My girlfriend told me to." I showed him how red really wasn't a good color for his skin, shared the mistake I'd made getting one once, and found a good blue shirt he would wear more than once to a party. Because I'd built rapport and as a Driver looking to hit goal, he also purchased a pair of boots and jeans—about $300 worth.

He returned to the store after he received a handwritten note from me thanking him for his purchase. He said, "You know, most people would have just gotten me the shirt and been done with it. But you took the time to educate me. Everybody said I looked so great that I should get more, so I'm changing my wardrobe." With that, he purchased thousands of dollars worth of clothes.

Low-hanging-fruit clerking would have been to clerk a $30 shirt.

Do you want to take money out of the business instead of put it in every month? *Sell* the merchandise; don't clerk it.

That can be hard, however, since many of us have had no formal sales training. I know I didn't. The manager of men's furnishings at the Broadway department store in Orange, California, where I worked in college gave me the most important advice in retail: "The customer is the most important thing. If you're doing something else and you see a customer, stop it immediately and go wait on him." That was great advice to hear, because it really made me aware of other people; however, I had no selling tools for what to do next. So I walked up to customers and said, "Can I help you find something today?" They always answered, "No, we're just looking." I'd respond, "Okay, if you need anything I'm right over here." I *hated* retail clerking.

I continued along this vein for many months. If I was lucky enough to have someone looking for men's Jockey underwear, for example, I could take them right over to the display and then suggest they get more than one pair. But for the bulk of the customers I met, I couldn't get over that initial rejection of "No."

Then one day, I realized that if I didn't want to get "No," then I probably shouldn't ask any question they could answer that way. I threw myself into product knowledge of everything we carried. Yet the results remained the same: lots of interactions with few rings of the register.

However, I discovered along the way that if I could find a way to get the customer to give me some information, I could find something we had in common and build trust. As I was developing this process to sell more merchandise, I read all of the Zig Ziglar and Tom Hopkins books about how to close the sale. As helpful as they were, I found that if I hadn't built trust to begin with, no "porcupine technique," "alternative of choice," or "reduction to the ridiculous" close could help me. I had to connect with my customers as people first and *then* as buyers. I had to find a way to get them to trust me from the moment I came in contact with them. That's when I created the Five Parts to a Successful Sale tool to consistently help myself; it became the single best tool I still use to turn a crew into a dynamic, involved, selling machine.

To succeed in retail, your mantra has to be, "It's different here, in a good way." And while that certainly starts with how your store is merchandised—the first words your employees utter are even more important.

Part One: The Greeting

There are five components to an effective greeting: the words, the speed, your intent, attitude, and ability to hit-and-run through the Hell Zone.

WORDS

The first element you want to get right are the opening words. "Good morning," "Good afternoon," or "Good evening, welcome to (name of your store)." That might sound a little formal for you, but you must make a conscious choice of words to prick up a new customer's ears to listen. *It's different here.*

If you know a returning customer by name, you can always insert it into the greeting or personalize it further. For example, "Hey Tom, how did Janie's audition for the musical go?" People love to know you know them. Customers are numb to the worthless greetings of, "Can I help you?," "Looking for anything in particular?," "How are you today?," and "If you need anything, let me know." Let your competitors ask them these tired questions over and over and hear, "No, just looking." Those greetings are placeholders in a conversation to which no one pays attention. Employees, ground down by so much rejection, numbly repeat them without thinking. And because customers hear the worthless greetings again and again, the employee is dehumanized. This opens the door to rude customer behavior such as talking on the phone at the register, price haggling, or unrealistic return demands.

Get the opening words right, and more often than not you'll hear customers say, "Thank you."

SPEED

From the thousands of mystery shops I've reviewed, I've learned that one of the things that bothers shoppers the most is how long it takes for someone to acknowledge them. The average time it takes to greet a customer in retail right now, *if it even happens*, is running around five minutes.

Do you know how long five minutes is? Take this simple test. Start the timer on your iPhone or BlackBerry as you walk in through your front doors. Continue through the whole store at a normal pace just like a customer and see how long five minutes is.

Five minutes is an *eternity*—especially if you're new to a store. Heck, 30 seconds is a long time! To stand out from your competitors, greet customers within 15 seconds. While that may sound like an extremely short period of time, it isn't. Use that same stopwatch or timer and repeat your walk through the store. In most cases, you can reach the back of your store within 15 seconds. You achieve three goals by greeting within this timeframe: you train employees to always have their eyes on who's coming in, you provide a welcoming atmosphere for the customer, and it also helps prevent stealing.

During the recent recession, customer theft went through the roof. The biggest deterrent to theft isn't security systems, locks, or devices; it's being noticed by an employee. With so many of your competitors not saying a word to customers for five minutes, if at all, shoplifters are more likely to steal from their stores rather than from somewhere where someone notices them.

Just as important as the speed with which we greet customers is the attitude that we have toward them.

Attitude

We've all heard about how Gen X and Y have few social skills, and while that may be true—*why* might this be? Could it be from all those years watching TV shows where even the five-year-olds make snide remarks to their parents? Could it be the lack of grandparents who had social skills to pass along concerning the right way to talk to people?

I don't know that for sure, but I do know one thing: It is up to *you* as the owner or manager to teach your crew the proper way to interact with other people, because they've never been taught by anyone else. And the attitude that they have before they walk up to a customer often makes the difference between, "Just looking!" and "I'll take it!"

I always do an exercise during my sales seminars where participants team up in pairs. I give them three scenarios that I ask that they
act out. The first is, "You are meeting the President or the First Lady
for the first time in the White House Rose Garden. How would you
greet them?" I look around the room and see people standing very
formally with rigid, outstretched arms while shaking hands, smiling
and polite.

The next example is: "You're at your brother's or sister's wedding. The person in front of you is either your new brother- or
sister-in-law. You've heard from your mother that they have committed many felonies, is probably only after your inheritance, and the
idea of this person having children makes you sick to your stomach.
How would you greet them?" I look around the room and see people
looking at their shoes, not facing the other person, looking away,
breathing shallowly, not giving him or her the time of day, barely
uttering the words.

The last question I ask is: "You're walking down the street and spot
your best friend you haven't seen in 20 years; how would you greet
them?" There are loud screams of excitement; arms flung wide open,
hugs, smiles and laughter.

What made the difference? Did the person in front of them suddenly grow horns and a tail? Did the person suddenly get minty fresh
breath? What changed? Someone usually gets it right away: "my attitude." *Exactly.* You thought the other person was a loser and treated
him that way. Or, you acted like best buddies and dropped all your
defenses.

While being cynical and judgmental can be fun when you're in
school and with peers, it is dangerous in business. Prejudging what
people can and can't afford is akin to shooting ourselves in the foot. I
employed an Expressive salesperson—who, when approached by a
frumpily-dressed customer who asked about a $400 beaded leather
vest, "How much is this?"—replied without thinking, "More than you
can afford." The customer hastily responded, "How do you know how
much I can afford?" The employee tried to cover up and back track a
bit by replying, "Because I saw all those shopping bags you were
carrying and figured you probably were maxed out." As an Expressive

personality, who tends to be able to smooth talk his way out of trouble when he gets caught, he was able to pull it off—*but just barely.*

They're All Purple and Their Money Is Green

Whether they are old or young, black or white, gay or straight, look homeless or own a million-dollar home, with kids or without, married or single—they're all purple and their money is green. If you can't train your crew to adopt this attitude toward customers, then you'll settle for bored, disengaged, or judgmental clerks.

Stewart was an employee of mine who thought he could tell who would buy and who wouldn't just by how they replied to him after he greeted them. After walking through the store with a potential customer, he would return to the counter area with his finger and thumb in the shape of an L for "loser" on his forehead. Nothing gave me greater satisfaction than going back and waiting on the guy, returning to the counter, and saying to Stewart, "Can you get me some boxes for his two pair of boots?"

Never let an employee decide who will and won't buy. It's usually the employee's own attitude from the outset that makes the customer decide to walk. Your initial contact needs to set people at ease, and that comes about from dealing with the Hell Zone.

More Than You Can Afford

I was in Morristown, New Jersey; a major home products company had paid me to train a large group of dealers. Marvin, the business owner of the host store, asked me to follow him through the showroom into the very back of the warehouse in order to have a private word.

He began, "I was in your class three years ago in Broomfield. Do you remember me?" I smiled but nothing came to mind. He

(continued)

(*continued*)

continued, "I enjoyed your session so much I came up to you afterward and asked, 'How much would it cost to bring you to my store?' *Now* do you remember me?"

I recalled the entire exchange, and saw it play out before my eyes. I had been full of my Driver self after completing the four-hour training session. Just as I was remembering him coming up to me at the end, he asked, "Do you remember what you said to me?" I sheepishly replied, "More than you can afford."

"How do you know how much I could or couldn't afford?" He had me; and he was right to call me on it. I felt like a fool.

It was probably the greatest thing anyone has ever done to teach me about sales. We make an ass of ourselves when we assume we understand how much value customers could get from our services—or how much they are willing to pay to get it.

Defeat the Hell Zone

The Hell Zone exists in every store, and is the first eight feet inside your front doors. I've given it this name because, well, no one likes being there. Customers don't like it because they'll inevitably be approached by an employee who says: "How are you today? Looking for anything particular?" The customer will then reply, "No, just looking," and will never see the employee again. Feelers, in particular, are put off by this hope for an interaction that is dashed.

Employees don't want to be in the Hell Zone because, in an attempt to be welcoming, they walk up to a customer and ask, "Looking for anything particular?" And the darn customer always responds, "No, just looking." After hours and days and weeks of this pattern, your employee gives up and says to herself, "I don't want that kind of rejection." So she says nothing and retreats to the counter to text on her phone.

Here's how to handle that awkwardness, engage the Feelers, and break this cycle.

GRAB A PROP

Grabbing a product—a book, a screwdriver, or a piece of clothing—gives your employee something to do that the customer will notice: putting away the item. This makes it look like the employee is interrupting something else to notice the customer, rather than swooping down on him like a hawk on a mouse. As the employee passes by the customer at about a 45-degree angle, he quickly greets and then moves past the customer. Most customers will appreciate having the space to look, and if they really need something, they'll stop the employee and request some help.

The technique of greeting with a prop puts the customer at ease, gives the employee a reason not to linger, and negates the Hell Zone. Here's how it works: A toy store employee picks up the LEGO pirate set and heads toward a customer within 15 seconds of the person entering the store. The employee approaches the customer at a 45-degree angle, starts to move past her with the prop, and pauses to meet her eyes and says: "Good morning, welcome to (name of your store). Feel free to look around, and I'll be right back." Done correctly and with the right intent, the customer always says, "Thank you."

Don't believe me? Try it right now; you'll be surprised. If they don't thank you, consider the fact that you may have approached at closer to a 90-degree angle, which blocks their path; you might have lingered too long during your comment; or you didn't look at them in the eyes. If the name of your business is too long, skip using it to make your greeting go quickly.

Why do you have to walk away and give them space? If a fly came into your house, you wouldn't immediately go running after it with a flyswatter. It's the same idea here. You want to return to the customer after he's been browsing for a couple minutes and make a positive statement about something he's looking at. Let's say that you saw someone in your hardware store pick up a Skil portable drill. You might say when you returned, "We have eight other portable drills right over here," and motion to another display. Your goal is not to "pitch," but to give information and space to browse.

The greeting tells the Amiable and the Expressive personalities, "I notice you, and you're valuable." For the Driver, the greeting provides a chance for him or her to find out if 'the salesperson is a player. For Analyticals, it can become part of a logical process to find what they're looking for and achieve a sale.

THE STORE TOUR

Store tours are a great way to show all that you offer in a concise way to new customers. Think of it like Disneyland: here's Tomorrowland, here's Fantasyland, and so on. You don't need to give too many details, just a general overview of what a customer will find in each area. You may want to start off by sharing some information about when your company started, who started it, and why. Your tour must include the following information:

1. Start at the front of the store and describe roughly five areas in a general way. Something employees in a Hunter Douglas Window Fashions Gallery might say, for example: "We begin with the mini blinds. Hunter Douglas was the pioneer in 1946 that came up with this product. We still make them today in a wealth of colors and different slat widths."

2. Consider following a timeline that describes when you added products due to demand. Ideally, you'll want to start with lower priced and end up with more expensive merchandise.

3. Keep your descriptions brief—maybe one or two sentences at the most.

4. Make sure to ask a question of the customer at the end. For example, "Did a couple of items catch your interest?"

5. Keep the whole tour under four—and preferably around two—minutes in length.

A store tour helps Analytical personalities borrow the "we can do this and this and this," from the Expressive personality, which keeps them from trying to "pitch" an item right away. It also helps prevent an Expressive customer from seeing something they hadn't considered while you are trying to wrap up the sale and throwing the whole transaction into chaos and uncertainty.

Brand Ambassadors

Tom Sullivan, founder of Lumber Liquidators, told me he witnessed a customer come in to their store in Florida because she
saw the perfect floor for their winter house during a store tour
where she lived in Boston. You don't know who a customer
knows or what other projects a customer may have knowledge
of, so use a store tour to help customers become brand ambas-
sadors and make you money.

Okay—so you've greeted the customer within 15 seconds, used
the right words, attitude, and with a prop. If she had a particular reason
for being there, you've allowed her to tell you. If not, you've walked
past her to an area in the store to put your prop down. After a minute
or two, you've returned to the customer and maybe given her a tour.
The way in which we greet people sets the stage for building trust. If
we don't build trust before we sell product, we are less likely to get the
sale—regardless of what personality type we are.

I was once given the chance to work with a young woman named
Rose who had such a great way with people. She was an Amiable who
could strike up a conversation about anything with practically anyone. Customers would go out of their way to return to Rose. As I
studied her early in my career, I realized she worked hard at becoming
someone's friend. And the more I studied it, the more I realized just
how easy it was.

One time, a customer entered the store and Rose asked how the high
school football team was doing. The customer smiled, told her about
the team and shared that she was a carpool captain. Rose explained that
her own kids' played the woman's children's team. She explained how
her carpool had grown so much that she had to get a new Chrysler
van. After she made the sale, I asked her how she knew the woman. She
said, "Oh, I didn't. All I had to do was look at her shirt, and there was
the insignia of the Canyon Country Cowboys. Because I knew the team
from my own experience, I was able to talk to her about it."

That got me thinking how many physical clues customers give us about what's important to them; they're right there if we take the time to notice. That's how I came up with Windows of Contact.

Part Two: Windows of Contact

When you walk down your street at night and notice your neighbors' windows are open, what do you do? (See Figure 4.2.) You look in and see what you have in common. That natural curiosity is what the second part of the sale is built on. That's different from how most people try to build rapport.

During the sales process, so many people—especially Amiables—think that just asking a bunch of questions makes them friendly. Nothing is further from the truth. How many times have you been approached by a needy salesperson who went on and on questioning you, firing one right after the other? It begins to feel like an interrogation

FIGURE 4.2   Windows of Contact Comes from Seeing What You Have in Common

or somebody punching a bruise after awhile. You instinctively want to say, "Get away from me!" Or even *worse*—the needy salesperson goes on and on about himself, his experiences, and how his life is great or sucks or whatever. No one likes that approach, either; it is a one-way street. To build the big sales, we need to establish a mutual foundation of trust. And that comes from being memorable.

I learned something early on about building trust; I realized that I, too, could be like Rose. It meant that I had to be a little smarter, think a bit quicker, and make myself a bit more vulnerable. I had to be willing to talk about something from my own life at a moment's notice. That's not something that comes naturally for Thinkers. I had to establish rapport and look for common Windows of Contact. These are physical and visual clues—including jewelry, clothing, a pair of glasses, a cell phone, car keys, insignia on golf shirts, shopping bags—anything unique to that person can be a Window of Contact. And the more detailed or unusual the item is, the better. The physical things are the windows that you consider going through. Make sense? The formula to remember is compliment, share, continue.

You need to sincerely *compliment* one specific item or aspect of the person—the window—then share something honest about yourself based on the individual's response. Use a good amount of detail without getting bogged down in a lengthy back-and-forth, and you'll quickly build trust.

The second step is to *share* something that you have in common with the window you've identified from the customer's response; it's like crawling through that neighbor's' window in Figure 4.2 and having a conversation. You found a window to help start the conversation. For example, if you noticed a beautiful gold tiger broach on a customer's lapel and complimented her saying, "I really like your tiger broach. Did you design it or purchase it?" She might answer, "It was a gift from my husband when he got a big promotion at work. He gave it to me over dinner after we saw the Siegfried and Roy show in Las Vegas—hence the tiger." The windows that opened during her response were: gift, celebration, memento, tigers, Vegas, Siegfried and Roy. That's all you could talk to her about, nothing but the clues you heard in her response. Got it?

So you search through your own experience. *Ever seen Siegfried and Roy?* No, I read about the accident; but that's not me. *Ever celebrated birthdays? Weddings?* Yes, but nothing memorable. *Vegas?* Then it hits you and you say, "I once rented a purple Dodge Prowler from Hertz at the Hilton and drove the Vegas Strip with the top down, then sped out into the hot desert one summer." You gave her enough detail to see your experience, and here's why that's so important: In a world of vanilla order takers, shoppers are looking to connect with memorable people. Even if they don't purchase from you that day, you need to find a way to stand out from the rest. And that's the magic of Windows of Contact, especially on higher ticket goods. The more detail you can share, the more memorable you and your store will be. But that only happens when you are honest about what you share; don't just try to make up what you think a customer wants to hear.

The share step is probably the hardest for most of us, because we were taught from an early age to never talk to strangers. Plus, we often don't feel like we want to open up to somebody, or we may feel that it's *not part of my job.*

Let me give you another example. A guy walks into your store wearing a T-shirt that says "Soccer Dad." A 10-year-old boy and a five-year-old girl accompany him. A stupid thing to say to him would be, "Oh, do your kids play soccer?" That would end with the customer either looking at you with disdain or a polite, "Yes" as he moved past you. What *could* you ask soccer dad to get him to talk to you? "Do you coach?" "What's the name of their team?" "Where do they play?" "What positions do they play?"—and countless other questions.

Soccer dad's answers will give you more windows you can talk to him about. For example, if he replied, "I coach my son's team, the Honey Bees, every Saturday morning down at Hart Park. We just had a game, and Johnny kicked the winning goal, so after this, we're going to In-N-Out Burger."

Did you notice the windows that soccer dad gave us? Hart Park, coaching, the Honey Bees, winning a game, and In-N-Out Burger. Those are the *best* things to discuss now with soccer dad. Coach made it memorable for you with all those details, so you'll have to make your reply memorable as well.

Let's take "winning a game" as our Window of Contact for this encounter. I want you to think of a time when you won a game—football, baseball, Scrabble, Bingo, you name it. Where were you, how old were you, and what made it memorable? Now, combine those details in a memorable sentence or two. For example, you might say: "When I played varsity football at Hoover High School, I once scored the winning touchdown. My dad let me get out of raking the leaves for a month because of it."

Notice how both of those exchanges were real and grounded in something that both you and this father did. This exchange was not long or complicated; but it did require that you think on your feet. That's incredibly powerful, because the more detail you can come up with, the more memorable you will be when that customer walks out your door. In a world of bland and blah, your story provides a hook. It's something to remember you and your store by that's unique to you. And people who can make these connections and tell these stories are exactly the kind of people you want on your sales team.

Now, I know that when you tell your crew to do this, your salespeople might react by asking, "Well, what do we do if there's a line at the counter?" Do it anyway. You'll learn when we get into training in Chapter 5 that we only train black and white—no grey. If you had replied, "If it's really busy, let it go," you would have as much as told them not to do it. Even when you are busy, it's just as important to connect with the customer as a person first, then make the sale. It is the one way to stand out for future visits. The world is full of Analytical order takers who think customer service is "getting them the product"; but it isn't.

You might also hear, "What if a customer comes in and I can't find anything to say?" That can certainly happen, but you can help your salespeople practice when you are on the sales floor by challenging them to come up with a story—even if they're just listening to someone else's customer. They can actively listen for potential Windows of Contact like a concert they went to, a neighborhood they moved to, and so on. While these statements naturally appear later in the sale—after the customer has dropped his defenses—it's more useful at this point in the sale—before you "sell" your products. Build rapport after the customer says, "I'll take it," and you've missed the chance to influence his purchase.

One year, during the week before Christmas, I was working at South Coast Plaza in Costa Mesa, California, at the western wear store I mentioned previously. I arrived at 9 A.M. to find a middle-aged guy waiting in front of the door. I looked at him and saw he was wearing a new goatskin jacket. (Anyone who's ever worked in western clothing has learned a lot about leathers; and one of things that makes goatskin remarkable is when it's brand new, it is very smooth, almost like plastic.)

I knew I had my Window of Contact as I had just purchased a new calfskin jacket myself. I approached him and said, "Good morning. Feel free to look around while I get the lights on, and I'll be right back." He thanked me, and after a couple of minutes I returned to him as he was picking up a pair of tan boots. I said, "That's a nice new goatskin jacket you've got. Was that a gift or did you buy it for yourself?" He put the boot back on the shelf, turned and said with a smile, "I bought it." I then said, "It's always nice to treat yourself. I just bought this Scully calfskin jacket yesterday because I've hit store goal for 10 years in a row. What was your reason?"

He looked at my jacket and replied, "The book I wrote has been optioned for a movie." Of course, the follow-up question I *had* to ask was: "What's the book?" He answered, "Ever hear of *The Hunt for Red October*? I'm Tom Clancy."

Would I ever have known who the renowned man in front of me was at that moment if I hadn't pushed myself to find some way into a conversation? No. If I hadn't been willing to put myself out there just a bit to get to know another person, I'd have missed out. You have no idea who the person standing before you at any given moment might be—a potential vendor, friend, partner, employee, famous writer— you name it. But you'll only find out by risking being memorable—in a *good* way.

The Windows of Contact method works well because it is a reciprocal interchange. I used hundreds of hot potatoes while training salespeople in Westminster, Colorado, on this technique. They paired up and had to find the window before they could pass the hot potato to the other person; an approach that emphasized the notion that this is meant to be a two-way conversation. Take too long and the potato burns your hands. When you find the window, you decide to go through it—and you both end up knowing a little bit more about each other.

Let's go back to the Feeler soccer dad's response: "I coach my son's team, the Honey Bees, every Saturday morning down at Hart Park. We just had a game, and Johnny kicked the winning goal, so after this, we're going to In-N-Out Burger." What if you ignored his response and simply said, "Uh huh. So what can I help you with today?"

You just disregarded the honest way in which he dropped his defenses to share with you; and you've just made your sales job twice as hard because you'll have to reestablish trust. When you say nothing after a customer shares, it's akin to slamming the window shut in his face, something no one, but especially Feelers, likes. Examine how you treated your customer every time you miss a sale; you probably lost it during this step, not at the end as you might assume. You have to change your personality during this crucial stage, not learn more canned "closing techniques" to spring on them at the end of the sale. Now that you're aware of Windows of Contact, see how many times people do that to each other in front of you today—and not just in retail.

Who will have the hardest time with the Windows of Contact? It's likely that the Thinkers will, because they're going to over think it. "What do I have to say?" "When do I do it?" "What exactly do I have to do?" They get caught up in the nuts and bolts of what is truly a simple interaction.

Amiables, on the other hand, will say: "Hey, I'm already doing this," and while in many cases they are, they are often doing too much or they may offer nothing about themselves. They also will say that because they don't want to be seen as doing anything wrong and will put a positive spin on anyone's performance, including their own. Expressives may share long stories about themselves or ask an excessive number of questions, thereby missing the back and forth. The formula of compliment, share, continue, keeps them to a snippet of conversation instead of a few minutes. Making it the second part of the sale, keeps Expressives from building the relationship after the purchase.

Keeping Windows of Contact short and sweet speaks to the Analytical's and Driver's need to keep interactions to the point. These types of customers might consider this exchange to be an intrusion, because they are on a mission. But that's precisely *why* it is such a valuable step. Windows of Contact are hardest for Analyticals to find, because they want to know exactly what to say each and every time. They are easiest for Expressive and the Amiable personalities to identify, because the Feelers are getting a chance to develop a relationship, something that doesn't come as naturally for Thinkers.

Share Something of Yourself

I instruct new franchise owners to have a team meeting where they give a short speech about why they purchased a franchise. One of them, Andrew, blew his crew away when he talked about waking up late after being at Yankee Stadium for a rained-out game against the Red Sox. He decided to go to work an hour late. He turned on the TV as he was getting dressed and saw the devastation of the Twin Towers. He said, "If I had gone to work that day, I would have been in the subway, right under the towers when they collapsed at 8:30. That day I decided to follow my dream of opening a bakery because life's too short. I'm glad you're here with me today." Those windows he opened and honesty of purpose were met with a great crew sharing of themselves freely, not just taking orders.

Since Windows of Contact sets the stage for the way in which your customers and employees talk to each other, mastering this practice won't just give you better sales—but a better sales *team* as well. Each of these windows builds a web of familiarity amongst staff members. You don't end up with silos of people just doing their own thing—like I recently encountered at my local Pottery Barn where seven employees stood motionless, silent, looking bored, and staring out into the mall. Employing the Windows of Contact technique can give you a vibrant team because they learn how to talk to each other as well as customers.

Part Three: Your Question

After establishing trust by greeting your customer like a friend and making yourself memorable using Windows of Contact, you want to ask one general question to get someone to tell you more about why he or she has' come to your store. If you're working in a toy store, it might be, "Who gets the gift today?" A hardware or fabric store employee might ask, "What's your project today?" A restaurant staff member could inquire, "What can we make for you today?" If you are a windows treatment store, it might be, "What room gets the makeover today?" You'll then use the information you learn from the customer from this stage during the last two parts of the sale.

Note, asking something like, "Are you looking for anything particular today?" and a customer answering, "a digital camera," misses the mark. It's not important that she's looking for a digital camera; what's important is *why* she is they looking for a digital camera. If a customer tells you that she's going on a trip, then you know that the camera's size is a significant factor for her. If she were shooting pictures of her son's track and field events, shutter speed would be the vital quality. If she liked taking close-ups of butterflies, then the zoom function would be the most critical feature. You want them to tell you freely how they will use the product, rather than you asking a hundred questions.

Getting the *why* information ahead of time means that the customer will be talking more than you. This makes you someone who is helping solve customers' challenges, not the aggressive salesperson pushing a product on them. This is the opposite approach of 90 percent of retailers out there—and one of the pillars upon which to build your business.

Think of this stage of the sale as a game. If you simply let a potential customer talk, he'll usually give you all the information you need to match up your products to his wants and needs and hone in on any additional items that could enhance his purchase. You're trying to figure out how all of your SKUs match up in an easy-to-understand way for your customer. Left to their own devices, Amiable customers, roughly 53 percent of the population, often can't decide so they say, "I'm just looking." Your goal in using one question is to capture enough information that you can narrow down their choices from all the merchandise you have to an easy-to-consider two or three.

Targeted questions like these allow Analytical salespeople to logically proceed through the sale. For example, "So you're going to create a new deck for barbecues with your family—you'll need this and this and this." Such questions provide Amiables with another chance to find out what someone is doing, something important to their natural curiosity, and the third part allows Expressives to come up with all the possible ways to solve a customer's challenge. Because Drivers innately look to fix things, such questions give them the chance to obtain the necessary information and come up with a solution.

After you've asked your question, the customer's answer should help limit choices. Much like the eye doctor's question during an eye exam, "Is one or two better?"—always give customers a choice. For example, Wisconsin-based Board Game Barrister owner Gordon Lugauer asks, "Do you want a strategy game, or do you not want to think?" Another of his questions during the third part of a sale includes: "Do you learn best by someone teaching you or by reading the rules?" While these might be too direct for a Feeler looking to create a family game night, they are perfect questions for a Thinker because they help to logically lock down the choices.

So many clerks assume that customers already know what product they want, but more often than not, they've just read a little online but are not wedded to a particular item. Most of your customers—especially the Feelers—are unaware of everything that's out there. That's precisely why they're standing on your sales floor. So if you haven't already, this may also be a good opportunity for you to give a store tour.

Now your customers need to know how and why your products meet their needs—in terms of specific features and benefits.

Part Four: Features and Benefits

You probably sell using features all the time, especially if you are an Analytical. But a lot of times we fail to ensure the customer connects the significance of a particular feature to the benefits the customer hopes to achieve; therefore, these attributes fall on deaf ears, resulting in lost sales.

In 1993, Cadillac came out with the new El Dorado, which I thought was a pretty sharp car. I walked into my local dealer and asked to see it. The salesman who greeted me said, "You know, it's got a Northstar engine." I felt stupid, like I should've done my homework before coming and even asking about that model. You never want to trip a customer's idiot switch.

The saleswoman who got the sale at another dealership told me during our exchange that it "has the Northstar engine feature, which means you only have to change the oil once every 10,000 miles."

In order to figure out what to point out as a feature's specific benefit, simply ask yourself, "So what?" And then answer it.

A feature generally starts with "It has," while you can introduce a benefit by saying, "so you." They must be connected somehow. For example, "This bottle of ketchup has an easy flow spout, so you don't have to take a knife and pull it out of the bottle." *Everything* has a feature and a benefit. Take a look at the pen on your desk. Is the cap on it blue? If so, what is the feature? That's right—it is blue on the outside. Now why is that important? So you know what color it is before you begin writing. Now link them together, "This pen has a blue cap on it, so you know the color of the ink before you start writing." Doesn't that feel more satisfying?

If I had just said, "This has a blue cap," you'd probably be wondering, "Why is he telling me this?" Or what if I had simply stated the benefit and said, "You know it's blue before you write." You'd be asking yourself, "How can he say that?" That's why the two must always be linked. Spout a laundry list of features—especially with technical words—and a Feeler's eyes will glaze over. You will have tripped the idiot switch and lost the sale—even if the customer continues to go through the motions.

Features and benefits must be meaningful to the *unique customer in front of you*—who you already know something about because you've built trust during the first three parts of the sale. One of the joys of working with Hunter Douglas was developing an intense advanced sales training program for its elite Gallery dealers. A specific feature that every attendee pointed out in role-playing was the childproof cords—a feature that only means something to customers who have kids in their house. If they don't, you've wasted precious time spouting the same generic feature and have, therefore, become quite unmemorable. Analyticals are most prone to use this cut-and-paste approach because they have catalogued all the features in their minds and are just waiting to share them with anyone—even customers who have no use for the information.

The best salespeople point out the *really* unique properties of a product that are not immediately recognized. A massage therapist might inform a client that she uses almond oil, a denser substance that helps to relax tired muscles. A shirt retailer might tell a customer that one specific brand uses a straight locking stitch on the hem, so that it doesn't unravel like a chain stitch can after several washings. Get the idea?

I was role-playing purchasing a barbeque at Sun West True Value in Arizona after training the staff on the Five Parts to a Successful Sale. I asked the salesman why one particular grill was $950, and he replied, "Home Depot has it for $50 less." I said to myself, "Great training, speaker boy"; as a Driver, I felt I'd failed. He quickly added, "But Home Depot charges you $20 for delivery, it takes a couple days to arrive, and you have to put it together yourself. We can deliver it assembled; and within a couple hours, you'll have a cold beer in one hand and be turning a steak over with the other." Perfect.

The Close

Will the customer buy it or not? Most sales training programs would follow the fourth part of the sale with "the close." There are hundreds of books written on how to close the sale, and you are probably already doing this in some form, anyway.

I don't spend a lot of time teaching how to close. If you did the other four parts correctly—you've been memorable in your greeting, built trust with Windows of Contact, figured out *why* the customer was looking for a solution to his problem with your items by using your one open-ended question, given him the features and benefits explaining why your product will do what he needs—then you should *assume* that he is buying from you.

Drivers, get out of the idea you can "make" someone buy with "just the right" closing technique. Even if they succumb and buy, they often return it or never come back, robbing you of the key to their wallet in the future.

Based on the customer's buying signs, the close can come in many forms. You could ask, "Do you want a box or a bag for this?" Or a customer might ask questions like, "How would I take care of this?" "Do you have layaway?" "What if I get it home and I don't like it?" A good salesman knows to stop selling and move on to Stage 5: the Add-on.

Even if there are no buying signs, you'll naturally move to the order at some point in the sale, If your customer says, "No, I have to ask my husband," you will need to go back and condense the reasons this product *would* meet her needs based on what you heard from her throughout the sale. I recommend at least three but no more than five points.

For example, a great salesperson in a window treatment store might say, "That's good. I just want to make sure I got everything correct. You said you were looking to redo the bedroom, that energy insulation was really important, that you need durability too because of your kids, and that this Silhouette window coverings is the right color." (Pause) "Is there anything else?" Then—*do not say a word*.

Thinker salespeople will want to control the silence; Feelers will hate any potential rejection and want to suggest something cheaper. Don't fold your tent! To all of you, I say: *Bite your tongue if you have to; the person who talks next determines the outcome of the sale.*

Poor salespeople repeat the negatives or bring up earlier objections that the customer has mentioned. Terrible salespeople drop the price or fold their tent, feel wounded,and sheepishly hand customers a business card and tell them to "Ask for me when you come back," which screams, "I'm on commission."

In a struggling economy, the higher the price of the item you're selling, the longer people may need to decide to part with their money for it. That's okay. If you know that you have built trust and provided a solution to the customer's problem, don't be afraid if she walks out the door. Do get her name, phone number, and e-mail address so you can follow up.

A Better Way to Use, "Anything Else?"

Linda Abrams Fleming, a salesperson with Haynes Furniture in Virginia Beach, Virginia, shared the following story about refusing to give up on a customer by asking one final question. "Yesterday, I engaged a woman who needed new carpet for her home. Her pet had passed away and the carpet needed replacing. The woman, Jane, had not shopped for carpet in over 10 years. We talked about her lifestyle . . . she had just retired, was on a fixed income, had a new puppy, and lived alone.

"Jane fell in love with three products, and I worked up an estimate. The price was about $4,200—much higher than she expected. I mentioned that we had interest-free financing for 36 months; but Jane wanted to pay for her purchase in full and avoid a monthly bill. We looked for alternative products that would be less costly, but she kept coming back to her original selections. Jane told me that she wanted to think about it.

"As I was getting out my business card, I asked her if there was 'anything else' concerning her about purchasing the carpet. She told me she didn't think she could move the books out of her bookcase and the curios out of her cabinets, and that because her children were scattered over the United States, she didn't have anyone to help her. I told her I would come over a week before the installation and give her a hand with moving her furniture. Jane replied by asking me, 'How much would it cost me?' and I answered, 'Lunch—peanut butter or tuna fish are my favorites.' She laughed, asked me again how much of a deposit I needed and got out her checkbook.

"There is a new type of customer out there: folks over 60-something with special needs. They have the time to shop, most often the financial means to purchase, and are usually looking for that 'connection.' As a result of my making a connection, I got the sale, helped a customer find the product that she wanted, and am doing something nice for someone. It's a win-win."

This is the essence of great retail: being of service to someone else. Help her to see that you have both the answer *and* the way to make her life better.

There's a better way to close a sale than trying to make someone buy. If you've followed the first four parts to a sale, you've built rapport and matched their products to their wants and needs; they'll signal you they want to take it home. After the customer has made up their mind for the main purchase, closing with an add-on finishes the job.

Part Five: Closing with an Add-On

You are ready to close with an add-on when you've heard the buyer say, "I'll take it" or have received other signals the customer is ready to buy. Instead of continuing to "pitch" the item, you are closing that sale by looking for an opportunity to get one additional item out the door. Often called "upselling," the second item must logically relate to the first, but you only want to present it *after* the customer has decided upon the main item.

For example, if you're selling a pair of $1,000 boots, an appropriate add-on would be the $25 shoe trees—not another pair of $500 boots or you'll throw the whole sale into chaos as the customer reconsiders the first item.

If you are selling a washer and dryer set, it would be the pedestals to stand the machines on to save the customer from hurting her back.

But you wouldn't try to sell the pedestals as the customer was trying to decide which washer and which dryer to purchase. Feeler customers would get overwhelmed with choices, shut down and say, "I can't decide" and walk out. This is particularly true of Amiables, because they focus on the salesperson's process instead of the products. So keep customers' choices simple with only one add-on.

If you are selling a car, it might be the iPod adapter for the radio system. A toy store could add the $20 rechargeable batteries that make the $75 toy run. Everything needs an add-on, but we don't want to create a laundry list.

MAKE THEM SEE IT—PAINT A PICTURE

To see how a good add-on plays in a sale, picture yourself at a restaurant in one of the following scenarios.

Scenario one: You've finished your dinner. The waitress comes up and says, "Anything else?" What did you see? *Nothing.*

Scenario two: The waitress comes up to you and asks, "Want anything else, like some cookies or ice cream?" You still don't see anything, so you probably respond with the same refusal.

Scenario three: After dinner, the waitress approaches you and says, "You know, we have an espresso brownie back there that I could warm up, drizzle a little of our creamy caramel sauce on top of, and add a dollop of whipped cream to; it goes really well with your coffee." Did you see it? *That's* the difference in closing with an add-on. You want to present one thing so well that you paint a picture of what it would be like to either enjoy now or to miss later.

Hardware stores frequently pride themselves on the fact that they have "old Joe," who can find the right nut for anything made since 1929. But I have news for you: You don't make money selling the 10-cent nut that goes on something from 1929. You make money on a customer who buys something new. So if you're selling a new drill bit set, why not close with an add-on by suggesting a new drill? Even though it is more expensive than the drill set, it does not compete for the sale of the drill bit set. Make sense?

A good salesperson constantly seeks the opportunity to suggest and build the sale, not close and leave the customer. If a nursery center customer is purchasing a tree in a five-gallon tub, the cashier should be suggesting the strong garden hose to water his new plant. If you sell lumber, why not talk about the need for a new blade for the saw? We have a misguided notion that the customer will automatically let us know if he needs or wants something additional. But that's Analytical-esque thinking, and nothing could be further from the truth.

The old saying "out of sight—out of mind" holds true here. After all, most of us don't hang out in our garage every day with our tools. We use them when we need them, and replace them when they break. If someone is getting ready to do a project, it is incumbent upon you as a hardware store salesperson to make sure he has everything he needs. You can do a point-of-purchase display by the molding that features the stain, masking tape, varnish, and so forth, but that's very passive. Instead of assuming that the customer has done his research and figured out exactly what he needs, teach your employees to close the sale with an add-on by walking the customer to the display after he's picked the molding. Again, we're tracking the number of units per sale by selling the merchandise, not clerking the low hanging fruit.

As you're looking to drive profits, the number one way is to raise the average check—and you do that by getting multiple items out the door. You can tell how good a crew you've got by noticing how well it can close with an add-on. You can present this to Drivers as a way to raise the average check and win the prize, to Analyticals as the logical things the customer needs, and to the Amiables and Expressives you are making sure customers have everything they need, like a trusted friend.

ADD AN ELEMENT OF FEAR

To make an add-on an even sharper picture, consider adding a bit of fear. For example, after your customer has selected five gallons of paint, you could say, "Have you ever gotten home and been ready to start a big job like this and realized you didn't have the right tools? We've got the angled trim brush that makes it go much quicker right over here." You convey to him the consequences of inaction; chances are that he'd rather get everything he can in one trip than have to return to the store midpainting.

UPSELLING AND YOUR CASHIERS

Putting cashiers in a sales mind-set requires some skill on your manager's part, because most cashiers fear and resist upselling. Why? Because they are probably the least friendly of your crew, so you "stuck them" on the register. If you catch them not doing it, they'll usually say something like, "No one wants it," or "I forgot." Adding on to every sale involves training your crew to think differently about selling, and the key to doing this is to get your crew to suggest other products in terms of simply offering an "additional service." This approach can go a long way toward breaking down a cashier's resistance to sales.

While you don't want to go overboard with this, here are a few ways to persuade your cashiers to engage in upselling:

1. Schedule enough employees during a given shift. Cashiers will not upsell anything if it means it might slow down the line.
2. Spend some time with cashiers before they hit the floor, so they know what is selling and what could be suggested. If you are a farmstand and your bakery plans to have a lot of French bread baking and fresh basil is readily available as well, convince the cashier to suggest that the customer purchase some basil or tomatoes to make an easy bruschetta appetizer. If you own a coffeehouse, train your cashiers to ask everyone who comes in on Christmas Eve or even Christmas if they have coffee for their holiday dinner.
3. Set goals to keep them motivated. You can track this by average number of units per customer on your POS.

Sales Autopsy: What if They Didn't Buy?

If you're having a tough time with a sale, pull back and see if you may be trying to sell to an Expressive like she were an Analytical—which doesn't work very well. Focus on what went on during the sale with your personalities, not the products.

A friend of mine named David visited a furniture store and told the salesman he was looking for a couch. Being an Amiable, David was patiently listening to the guy tell him everything about how the wood was chosen, the Dupont fabric that resisted stains, the strength of the steel springs, and the additional no-tax discount. The information overwhelmed David, tripped his idiot switch, and prompted him to inform the salesman that he'd have to think about it. The guy said to him, "What's wrong with you, are you sick or something?" All David needed to know was how the couch would fit in his house, and the Analytical salesperson was giving him *far* too much information.

Existing Employees Require More Explanations

Your goal from the beginning is to welcome customers with a unique greeting that gets their attention, introduces you as an employee, and puts them at ease. However, the idea of one standard greeting might become a sticking point as you train existing employees on the Five Parts to a Successful Sale—especially if you have Expressives who want to "do it their own way," or Amiables who are comfortable with what they are doing and naturally fear change. Their pushback can make you feel like you are stuck looking at the rock in the mud instead of getting up in the blimp and looking down on what you are trying to achieve: an exceptional experience for your customers.

Your greeting to someone you do not know, to be taught to all employees as the only acceptable greeting during their six stages of training, is as straightforward as: "Good morning (afternoon or evening), welcome to (Name of your store)." Pause. "Feel free to look around, and I'll be right back." This is ideally delivered with a prop, so that you can greet, walk away, and let the customer browse without feeling you are "pouncing on her." Again, you should deliver your greeting sometime within 15 seconds of customers entering your store—not so slowly that they wonder if anyone noticed them, or that potential thieves assume that no one is watching them. But it shouldn't be so quick that they walk in the door and you spook them.

You have to train in black and white: at the beginning, there is only one way to do it. It's like your response to a four-year-old who reached up to touch the stove while you were cooking: "Don't *ever* touch the stove." But after he gets older, he learns that there is a gray area; once he sees the knob is off, he can touch it. Similarly, after your employees have been trained, gray is permissible. If they know the customer by name, they should feel free to use something like, "Good morning (first name). Great to see you again," and so on. If, for instance, your employee recently helped the person find a gift for a birthday purchase, it would be appropriate to ask something like, "How did the birthday party go?"

Can you script every single interaction? No; and you don't want to. You *don't* want the generic or formula greetings that untrained employees in competitors' stores use like, "Hi, how are you today? Let me know if you need anything," or "Hi, looking for anything special?" These are forgettable and often results in customers saying, "No," ignoring your employee, walking past him, and ultimately treating your employee poorly.

How do you know if your greeting worked? Customers will interact with you. Your goals for the greeting are:

♦ Welcoming customers as you would welcome someone to your home.
♦ Making clear that they aren't in just *any* store, but your store.
♦ Putting them at ease.
♦ Letting them know you are there for them.
♦ Conveying the fact that they have time; you aren't going to push them.

If this greeting is done correctly, 90 percent of customers will automatically reply, "Thank you." If they don't, it might be because the person delivering the greeting did not connect with the customer's eyes. This means that your employee is talking to the customer's back as she walks away—leaving him with no response. That doesn't feel particularly good for anyone but especially the Feelers.

Your goal is obviously not to be some type of parrot, or to make your employees into robots. It's *just the opposite*. You want to meet customers so they thank you, not shun you. Then you can begin to create an exceptional experience for them. Don't worry about the fact that they'll hear you repeat the same greeting over and over. This is not about you; it is about your customer. You need to reinforce the idea that for the next three to seven minutes—or however long the customer visits with you that day—that this unique customer is the *most important thing for you to attend to.* Customers should feel no bias or cynicism—nothing but open arms. That can't happen if you have Expressives thinking customers will notice them repeating the greeting or Analytical employees focused on "what-ifs." These are what I call the rock-in-the-mud details; you want to encourage them to be "up in the blimp" looking down at the big picture to engage the customer.

We repeat things to people all the time, often without thinking. Happi Olson explained it this way to her crew in Minneapolis, "Think of hosting a big party. When someone arrives you might say, 'Welcome! So nice to see you (name of guest)!' Pause. 'Feel free to put your coat down on the bed in the room to the right; drinks are in the kitchen, and I'll be right with you.' The next guest arrives, and you say the same thing. Why? Because you are giving each person the information they need in order to relax and have a good time."

There are a variety of "what-ifs" that you might imagine. What if the person interrupts you and just demands something or asks a question before you give the greeting? That's fine; just leave the greeting off. What if five people walk in together; do you greet each one individually? Probably not; but you could address the group with your usual greeting, and they would appreciate it.

Analyticals will ask, "What if you are slammed?" or "What if someone else greets them?" What if they . . . ? What if? *What if*? Every job requires a lot of judgment calls. You can't micromanage every instance; spending time imagining every potential customer interaction serves no one well, *especially* our customers.

Once new employees master your one black-and-white greeting, you're bound to hear how easily it gets results. Existing employees' attitude toward the greeting often determines the success of your training program. Though this isn't something you're forcing on them to frustrate them, some personalities will get this impression.

The challenge here is that we perform to the level of our fears. Employees who fear being fired for not using your greeting to the letter will subconsciously set themselves up to fail—particularly the Feeler personalities. The reason you adopt a selling system is because you want to be profitable. But this doesn't come across when you let employees ignore customers or simply say, "Can I help you?" when they enter your store.

Fighting, questioning, mocking, or worse—ignoring—the sales process weakens your company. The fight for the consumers' dollars has never been greater, and it doesn't do anyone an ounce of good to hold onto negative energy. As you train the Five Parts to a Successful Sale, remain focused on your goal to create an outstanding experience for every single potential customer you meet.

Testimonial: The Five Parts to a Successful Sale

While writing this book, I received this note from Meghan Gardner, a former colleague, that speaks to how effective the Five Parts to a Successful Sale can be:

"I was a manager at the busiest It's A Grind Coffee House in Long Beach, California. Our crew rocked and served several hundred customers every morning. We knew all of our customers, made drinks fast, and made great money in tips—all while having a [fantastic] time at work. I eventually became a bit cocky about the success of the store and our customer service ability.

"Then one day, the owner brought in Bob Phibbs as a consultant. All I thought was, 'What the hell?! We don't need *anyone* to tell us how to do better with customer service! Just watch our store; it's obvious that we're [just fine].' As a result, I expressed a snotty, know-it-all attitude to Bob during our first training encounter. I [made it clear that I] didn't need or want his advice. My crew [felt] pretty much the same way; we weren't exactly ready to think positively of any possible change.

"What I didn't realize at the time was that, while in reality our store was pretty darn good from the customer service side, we had never really considered some of the additional sales aspects of Bob's selling system. I continued to resist his lessons, even though other stores saw their average ticket rise as a result of using the system. Then I got promoted.

"Our company started to grow, and [badly] needed a training department. Now *I* was responsible for incorporating Bob's training into our program—and even teaching it myself. I had an 'ah-ha!' moment when I started to realize that while we previously might have hired some people who were naturally talented at talking to people and upselling, that was the exception—not the rule.

"From that moment on, it just clicked. I was able to train Bob's system because it formalized much of what I did naturally. It sunk in that no one, including Bob, was expecting 100 percent of the transactions to sound the same and rehearsed; but that each individual made the sales system work while inputting his or her own personality in it.

"Once I realized how valuable Bob's training is—and how essential it was to keep a company growing consistently—my respect for him grew. The funny part is that although I'm no longer in a career that most people would consider customer service, I still use Windows of Contact every day! This training of how to develop trust is currently at work in my current career as a police officer."

I've alluded several times to what is *not* to be tolerated on a sales floor. Listed below are the three *worst* questions to ask (in addition to "Anything else?" which we covered previously) and one answer you *never* want an employee to give—in *any* business.

The Worst Questions and Response
"How Are You Today?"

Does anyone really care? *No.* And chances are that the person asking isn't really ready to be a shoulder to cry on if we're having a tough day. It's like that line in the country song "Lookin' for Love": "I'd turn to a stranger just like a friend." Some people will politely play along and say, "Fine, how are you?" and you might answer with another pleasantry. But no matter what your personality, when the other person doesn't answer, you feel rejected. Time is precious; don't take it up with a placeholder like this question.

"CAN I HELP YOU FIND ANYTHING?"

I always want to answer, "Several million dollars." The danger in asking this is that it feeds right into the mission shopper mentality of the Thinkers who know exactly what they're looking for. But the profit comes from their browsing.

"DO YOU WANT ME TO PUT THIS UP AT THE REGISTER WHILE YOU LOOK AROUND?"

Mission shoppers will say, "No, that's all." It's preferable to avoid this question and merely say to the customer, "I'll put these up front and be right back."

"NO PROBLEM"

Okay—this isn't really a question. But telling a customer that something is "no problem" negates what you went through to make that person feel special. For example, let's say a front desk agent at an upscale hotel told a regular customer as he checked in, "I was able to upgrade you to the Presidential suite and included a dozen roses for your anniversary." When the customer said, "Thanks—that's great! I really appreciate it," an appropriate response would be, "We've valued your visits here for years. If there's anything that I or any of the staff can do to make your visit better, we're here for you."

Now, what if, instead of that statement, the front desk agent replied, "No problem"? That elevates the employee's role above the customer, and diminishes the importance of the customer's loyalty in making this stay exceptional. The retail salesperson's role is to put himself *second* to the customer. The message coming to the customer when you say "No problem" is: "No skin off my back. Don't think I had to go through anything for you. I mean it's only *you*; I'd do the same for my dog."

I have been saying for a while that it's time we got rid of the words "customer service," because no one even knows what it means. Using the Five Parts to a Successful Sale keeps you focused on the customer and puts your needs and personality second. This is easy to measure because it shows up in the bottom line of your financials.

Okay, so let's review the Five Parts to a Successful Sale.

The Greeting
◆ Welcome customers like they're coming to your home.
◆ Use the right words: "Good morning, good afternoon, or good evening."
◆ Have a positive, friendly attitude.
◆ Greet them within 15 seconds, but do give them some time to enter.
◆ Use a prop to defeat the Hell Zone.
◆ Offer a Store Tour where appropriate.

Windows of Contact
◆ Find something that you can talk to them about and build rapport, trust, and the sale. That's the window.
◆ Share something honest about yourself. Blow this, and you're going to get objection after objection at the end—because your customer simply won't trust you.

Your Question
◆ Use the one question that is asked of everyone to help get information as to *why* and *what* the customer is trying to do. This approach works much better than trying to pin the customer down on a specific item, and, like a vending machine, grabbing it, delivering it to him, and having him pay at the cash register.

Features and Benefits
◆ Precede the feature with "It has."
◆ Explain the benefit in the same breath, so that customers understand how the product relates to their needs. If, for example, a wife purchases a $4,000 hot tub as a gift, she knows the triple-insulation is better because it saves money versus the other competitors' brands—and can tell her husband to justify the price.

Closing with an Add-on

- Paint a picture so clearly that the customer sees the benefits of the product before purchasing it.
- Help customers see the results of *not* getting the full benefit of their first item unless they buy the add-on.

When we do all of this, everyone wins; customers get more of what they really wanted because we made the effort to get it right, we had a helpful attitude, and we grew sales.

STAT: Five Things to Do Immediately after Reading This Chapter

1. Try to greet someone without asking, "How are you today?"
2. Find a Window of Contact to compliment, share, and build a relationship with a customer or employee in the next 30 minutes.
3. Point out a feature and a benefit of the next product a customer asks a question about.
4. Take your number one bestseller and try to come up with five add-ons.
5. Listen to how many times you or your crew uses the worst questions or response in a day, then work to correct this.

Chapter 5

Clone Yourself to Train Effectively

According to Dr. Holly Carling, the human body breaks down and replaces over 24 billion cells a day to ensure that it functions as designed. If the cells are not replicated exactly, they mutate, which can cause cancer. A similar type of "retail cancer" can take place in a store where we find people on the floor with minimal training. This leads to meaningless interactions with customers, boredom, and wasted time, money, and profits. Staff members—who know all the *don'ts* but never got the *do's*—lack sufficient training, which lowers the bar on making sales and delivering exceptional service.

I can recall one particular time when I questioned a manager as to why he hadn't gotten rid of an employee, and he told me, "Because she's really great when I'm there." But truly great employees do the right things when you *aren't* there—as a result of their training and the way in which you brought them into your organization. An important point to keep in mind: you're only as good as the person you left in charge while you went to the bank.

So how can you ensure that your employees function as you want? The answer is to clone yourself by using written job descriptions to illustrate your expectations, a handbook for all the *don'ts* of your business, and a training program that covers all your *do* procedures. A job description should contain action words like *teach*, *sell*, and *train*. Because you probably already have an employee handbook that details everything in black and white, we'll skip that. Instead, this chapter includes checklists about what to cover for the trainer as well as for the trainee. We'll give examples of phone scripts, customer interaction, and follow-up calls. Along the way, we'll discuss the needs of each of the four personalities again. Finally, we'll train the trainer with necessary skills and discuss what to consider when promoting or dismissing employees. We'll also show you how to create your own training program by breaking everything necessary to drive sales into bite-size modules.

When I was 15 years old and had first joined the United Methodist church youth group in Pasadena, California, a bunch of us decided to "TP" our classmate Jane Lindley's home. We drove up quietly and each of us grabbed a handful of toilet paper rolls and proceeded to hurl them into the palm trees, through the bushes, and all over the lawn. Just before leaving, I turned on the sprinklers.

As we piled back into the VW microbus one of the guys said, "Who turned on the sprinklers? That was really mean." *Oops.* I thought I was *supposed* to be mean, but since no one told me *why* we did it in the first place, I just relied on my instincts, which, evidently, had been misguided.

That's why we have to train people thoroughly—so that they understand the *why* behind the reason that we do the things we do, and not, like a Driver or Amiable just assume they'll get it. I'm sure some of you are saying, "My people have been with me forever, Doc. They don't need training; they already know it all." If you haven't had a training program before, things have happened because people had to try to figure out how to make it work. That doesn't make it the right way, the best way, or the most profitable way; just the way you've always done it.

Where to Start?

Much like you did in Chapter 3, start by considering your desired outcomes as well as your own pet peeves in order to shape your training program. Begin by recording everything you think a new employee should know about your business in these four categories:

1. **Procedures.** The how-to information that includes ringing up a sale, clocking in, and providing an exceptional experience for customers.

2. **Policies.** The do's and don'ts of your business—including rules for smoking, phone calls, dress codes, and so forth.
3. **Product knowledge.** The specifics of your merchandise—why you carry it, in what ways it is better than the competition, who tends to buy it, and so on.
4. **Sales.** How to sell your merchandise.

Pet Peeves

Your training must also cover the things you absolutely want to avoid in your business. For example, one of my pet peeves is when employees stay clustered behind the counter. They are like bees in a beehive daring someone to come over and be stung. I experienced something like this recently at a Home Depot when I was looking for assistance with some backsplash tile. I discovered three male employees standing around a workstation desk and a fourth employee sitting back in her chair, chatting about the lack of customers, I think.

I came within 10 feet of the desk and the group kept talking. The female employee remained tilted back in the chair looking at me. No one said a word.

"Excuse me," I said. "Can I get some help?"

Without moving, the woman said, "What are you looking for?"

"There's something over here. . . . "

She jumped in, "Well, what is it?"

I blurted out in frustration, "I don't know what it's called, but if you would get off your butt, I could show you." (Oops—there's that Driver impatience.)

She got up and moved toward me and I led her back to the display. I began to feel bad as I explained what I needed and said, "Sorry, I didn't mean to say that." Even Drivers have a heart.

She replied, "That's okay. People often don't get what we're saying."

I don't think she knew what *I* was saying. It's not up to the *customer* to respond correctly. The employees should have broken up their group and immediately approached me with an offer to assist. Instead, they stayed in their pack, making the customer, who was trying to spit out the correct name of the product, increasingly less comfortable.

I still can't recall the name of that backsplash tile, but I do recall with clarity my own laid-back, customer-ignoring behavior from more than 20 years ago. I was just out of high school and working at the Nunn Bush Shoe Shop in the Glendale Galleria. I was talking to my boss behind the counter while a customer looked through all the shoe displays. Instead of ending our conversation and talking to the customer to assess his needs, we kept right on talking.

Finally, the customer came up to us and asked, "Is this all you have?" I guess I was feeling my oats that day when I said, "No, we have three floors above us. We want people to guess what we have."

The customer quipped, "Next time, take your bad mood out on somebody else!"

I wish I could say I was put in my place and immediately gave him the attention and apology he deserved. But it wasn't until later that I realized why and how I'd truly been a jerk that day. I think it started when I allowed a wall to come between the customer and myself. I considered myself to be this great resource, so great, in fact, that people would approach *me* and request my help. That's a Thinker personality for you.

While I couldn't salvage that shoe shopper's experience, that incident stayed with me for a long time as an example of how *not* to behave behind the counter. And because of that experience, one of the most important points I make in my training is not to allow employees to cluster like somebody has racked them up. When they see a customer, they should immediately scatter.

Stand Out with Scripts

Creating scripts for repetitive situations ensures that your entire staff meets your expectations for your store tour, answering the phone, or how to take a deposit from a customer on a custom order. There's not a lot of room for error when you're training a scripted interaction. As your employees (and you) get comfortable with your script, you're free to expand, personalize, and so forth. But to start off, here's how to create a phone script to add to your training and will set you apart from competitors:

1. Identify **where** the person called.

2. Identify **the person** to whom the caller is speaking.

3. Initiate the **conversation.**

4. **Presell** the customer on your products.

5. Ask for **permission** to continue.

6. Suggest the customer bring in **materials** to make a visit more productive.

7. Cover your three most frequently asked **questions**.

The following is an example of a phone script I created for a Hunter Douglas store:

You: Thank you for calling (name and location of your store). This is (your name) speaking; how can I help you?

Caller: "I want to get someone to come out to my home and give me a quote for window shades."

(While your competitors would gladly give him or her an appointment, you want to be different, so your script would continue in the following way.)

You: "While we can do that, we work a bit differently. May I tell you about it?" (You always want to ask for permission throughout a phone call to give the customer control; 95 percent of people will say "Yes.")

You: "We are one of only 400 Hunter Douglas Window Fashions Galleries in the world, which means that you can come to our showroom and see all the products Hunter Douglas makes installed in actual windows. We have found that customers who visit our showrooms are much more comfortable in making the right decision for their window coverings. Once you have picked out a few, then we can bring the smaller samples out to your home. How does that sound?" (Again, most people will say something like "good," which you can follow with, "May I set up a time to show you our gallery?")

Do you see how that phone script shows the customer exactly how your business is different? It raises his or her expectations and makes you stand out from the other people the customer calls for an in-home appointment.

A phone script works for any type of business, from an outdoor furniture retailer to an appliance store. Because a phone call can be your first contact with the customer, you want it to be perfect every time. There are many more procedures and scripts you can develop that give specific direction on what to say when doing things like juggling customers or following up with personal thank-yous.

Back to Your Training List

When you have at least 10 specific points under Procedures, Product Knowledge, and Sales with which you're satisfied, prioritize them into an order that builds from the basics to the most advanced over six stages of training. For example, you don't want to tell trainees to price games until they know where the games are in your store, where the price sheets are kept, and where the price gun is located.

Your list of specific points is meant to jog the trainer's memory and allow him to teach precise procedures, relate stories, and share examples. After you have all of your stages written, decide if you've missed anything major and add that in. You should also remove any insignificant items.

It is incredibly hard for new hires to be asked to do things on which they haven't been thoroughly trained. For instance, it's common practice for store owners to start new employees as cashiers when they don't know the products or the register. A coworker steps up to the counter to help and tells the customer, "Sorry, she's new and doesn't really know what she's doing." This is very embarrassing for any employee (especially Thinkers). In another instance, a manager might expect an employee to have been trained, finds that he hasn't been, becomes irritated, and asks, "Don't you know that?"

A simple way to avoid those frustrations is to use a series of training badges.

Training Badges

Training badges are used at certain stages of instruction to keep new employees from being asked to do too much. For example, a red badge might mean, *"Don't ask me to do anything. I am brand new, and I don't know how anything works yet."* After a series of trainings and a product knowledge test, the employee gets a yellow badge that signifies: *"Caution: I know some things but still not very much."* The green badge at the end of a successful training means, *"Yes, I can do it all, but it might take me a bit longer."* You'll find a template online (details at the end of the book) that you can duplicate on red, green, and yellow paper. Badges also allow customers to see which employees are new hires and cut them some slack.

The next section will review the six stages of training and give you lists you can use to build your own program.

The Six Stages of Training

You need to balance the breadth of training with what an employee can process in one stage, the opportunity to achieve mastery, and the employee's schedule. There is not an absolute figure or rule, such as, "Within six days, new employees need to show they have learned everything in a given stage." Depending on individual employees, mastering a specific stage could take a day—or a week. If you are training part-timers, it could take a full month.

Analyticals are drawn to training because of the black and white nature of the process, so make sure that your trainer approaches the process with the goal of teaching, not checking off boxes next to items. Training should initially focus on helping the student to become comfortable; the trainer finishing his job is secondary.

Use the following sample six stages training list as you build your own training program. You'll notice I teach Part Three: Your Question before Windows of Contact, because it is easier for new employees to do successfully. Everything needs to be taught exactly as it should be done; shortcuts by trainers or other employees must not be permitted. Give staff members an overview of what you will be covering in that day's training, and make it as detailed as you can with specifics just for your business.

Training Stage One

Give new employees an overview of what you will be covering in that day's session. For example:

"This stage is to get all the paperwork completed and to learn the rules and procedures. We'll be working to make you comfortable with meeting people. You will be able to self-direct to keep our store clean and tidy and be able to greet every customer in a welcoming manner."

Employee Introductions

◆ Introduce trainees to employees with whom they will be working so they feel comfortable in their new environment.

◆ Make sure to introduce managers or assistant managers by their title and explain briefly what they do.

Check All New Employee Information

◆ Use an orientation form to make sure that new employees have read and signed all information. Give them a copy of your Employee Handbook and have them sign it as well to express their understanding of it once they have had a chance to read it.

◆ Show how to clock in on the register.

◆ Explain dress code.

◆ Issue name badge.

Store Tour

◆ Show new employees where everything in the store is (this should take no less than 15 minutes and no more than 30).

◆ Start with the front of the store, as a customer would, and move to the right in a counterclockwise path. Highlight general areas, not specific products.

The Counter

◆ Explain that employees are only to remain here to ring up a sale; they are never to stand behind it, waiting for customers.

♦ Be sure they understand employees are to scatter from behind the counter when customers come in.

Training Badges
♦ Review different badges in accordance with the completion of each stage.
♦ Explain that the badge system is for their benefit as well as the customer's (since people are usually nicer and more forgiving when they know that someone is new).

Sales Training Part I: The Greeting
♦ Explain that the policy is to greet every customer within 15 seconds of his or her entrance, to be friendly and welcoming, to speak in a loud enough voice to be heard, and to look the customer in the eye.
♦ Let trainees know they should feel free to call customers by name if they know them.
♦ An acceptable greeting for customers you do not know is, "Good morning (afternoon, or evening), welcome to (name of your store). Feel free to look around and I'll be right back."
♦ Unacceptable greetings are: "How are you today?" and "Looking for anything in particular?"
♦ Explain to your staff that if someone (or several people) is waiting at the counter, employees are to look them in the eye and say, "Hi, I'll be right with you," so the customers do not get upset.
♦ Explain how to juggle more than one customer.
♦ Remind staff members to ask customers for permission to leave if they must and to thank customers for waiting upon their return.

Cleaning Procedures
♦ Go through every point under this heading in detail. Show new employees exactly what needs to be done and where all items necessary to complete the task are kept.
♦ Review thoroughly each item on any cleaning checklists.

◆ After you have trained staff members, have them perform all the activities on the list again by themselves.
◆ Check all work and correct anything that is not done to your satisfaction.
◆ All Stage One cleaning must be done throughout the day and anytime an employee starts a shift.

How To's
◆ Use the script to answer the phone.
 • An appropriate greeting: "Thank you for calling (name of your business), this is (your name), how can I help you?"
 • The maximum number of rings allowed before a staff member must answer.
 • How to place a call on hold; instruct that they ask the customer's permission prior to doing so. Return to a caller on hold and thank her for holding.
◆ Give directions to the store using landmarks, for example, "Fifth and Main outside of Macy's by entrance B."
◆ Gift wrapping.
◆ Stocking shelves and back rooms.

Before the trainees leave, give them positive feedback on the job they did—even if everything didn't go 100 percent as planned. Make sure to collect all information and have them sign off on their orientation checklist. Ask if they have any questions. Go to the schedule and have the employees copy their training schedule for the week. Confirm when you will see them next.

Stage Two Training
Give your employees an overview of what you will be covering in today's training by letting them know that they'll be learning additional store operations as well as more sales training in this stage. You should also give them a training packet and an assignment to learn after this stage.

Review and Repeat
◆ Have new employees complete all Stage One cleaning procedures on their own after clock-in.

♦ Make sure employees understand everything that was covered during the previous stage of training, and ask for any questions.

Product Knowledge

♦ Train your top five categories and at least three products in each.

♦ Try to include an activity where they have to find products on the shelf, locate accessories, and so on.

Sales Training Part III: Your Question

♦ Explain that your business uses one particular question because you want the customer to provide you with clues on how you can help. Explain that your goal is for employees not to be order takers who ask what customers are looking for and then get it for them; this approach will never allow the customer to discover all that your store can deliver.

♦ Once the one question is asked, let the employee help a customer with her decision by inquiring with more open-ended questions about her needs, where and how the item or service might be used, and so forth. From there, have the employee suggest one of his own favorite items. If he doesn't have one, teach him what the most popular items are so that a new hire can say, "We sell a lot of _____."

♦ Give training packet homework that includes 10 categories, products, or services you offer. Explain to your employees that before you begin the third stage, they will have to pass a quiz on these materials. If they don't, they will need to go home and study further to retake the quiz. Ask if they have any questions, and confirm when you will see them next.

Stage Three Training

Give your staff members an overview of what you will be covering in today's training. Explain that the test covering the homework packet will be given and if your employees score at least 80 percent, you'll continue teaching the process for building trust with your customers.

Review and Repeat

◆ Have new employees complete all Stage One cleaning procedures.

◆ Make sure employees understand everything that was covered during the previous two stages of training. Ask if there are any questions.

Category Homework Test

◆ Administer the homework test, which the employee must pass with a score of 80 percent or better.

◆ Grade the test so that the answers meet your satisfaction. If employees do not pass, you should send them home and reschedule Stage Three for another day.

◆ If they pass, trade red In Training badges for yellow ones.

Sales Training Part II: Windows of Contact

◆ Explain the formula of compliment, share, and continue. Remind your employees that we want to notice something unique about the person in front of us, share something of ourselves based on that person's response, and continue to build a relationship with him.

◆ Some examples of common windows are things you can see: hairstyle, clothing, jewelry, cell phone, car, and so on. Asking someone if he saw the game, however, is not opening a window, because he could say "No."

◆ Make sure your employees understand that the idea is to create a conversation, not simply ask a lot of questions. They want to converse with customers by sharing information about themselves that relates either to what they originally complimented the customer on or any insight they obtained from the customer's response. This way, customers get to know the staff and look forward to returning to the store.

◆ Using Windows of Contact also makes work more fun because we get to know more about each other, a little bit at a time.

Thanking

◆ Even if the customer doesn't buy anything, make sure employees know they should look the customer in the eye and thank her for coming in. They should never say thank-you to a customer's back as she is leaving.

◆ If a purchase does take place, the employee comes around the counter and hands over the purchase with a thank-you, encouraging the customer to return again soon.

Post Test

◆ Give an oral quiz and ask new employees about a few products of your choice from the day's training.

◆ Again—compliment the trainees on their efforts that day before they leave, even if everything did not go perfectly well. If you will be giving them a product information test before moving on to Stage Four, give them the training materials for 20 specific products. Ask if they have any questions. Confirm when you will see them next.

Stage Four Training

Again, let trainees know what you will be covering in that day's training. Remind them about the product knowledge homework test on which they need to score at least 80 percent before you can continue the training, which will cover describing merchandise to customers with an emphasis on features and benefits.

Review and Repeat

◆ Have new employees complete all Stage One cleaning procedures.

◆ Make sure employees understand everything that was covered during the previous three stages of training.

◆ Ask if there are any questions.

Product Knowledge Test

◆ Administer the product knowledge test (employees should have received the materials the night before).

- Employee must pass with 80 percent or better. Grade so that answers meet your satisfaction. If employees do not pass, they should clock out, and Stage Four should be rescheduled for another day.

Continued Product Knowledge Training

- Train employees on the products on which they were tested. Include role-play, using the items, and discussing which customers would find value in them.

Sales Training Part IV: Features and Benefits

- Remind employees that a feature is something you point out, and a benefit is the reason that it's important to the customer. We determine which features and benefits to present to the customer based on the insight he or she gave us after we asked our one question during the third part of the sale.
- Feature/benefit oral test: select 10 products from the store and have the employee give you the features and benefits of each.

Review the First Four Parts of the Sale

1. Greet everyone with "Good morning, good afternoon, or good evening, feel free to look around and I'll be right back." Return to the customer in a couple of minutes and make a positive comment about what he is looking at or open a Window of Contact.
2. Find Windows of Contact to compliment, share, and continue. Our goal is to build trust and openness with our customers by finding things in common.
3. We ask one question to get customers to talk about their needs.
4. A feature that starts with "it has" must be connected to a benefit for the customer with "so you."

Ask if your employees have any questions. Take them to the schedule and confirm their next shifts.

Stage Five Training

As always, give employees an overview of what you will be covering during training that day. Inform them that this stage is dedicated to register training and a review of customer service. Provided that this stage's training test is passed, a green In Training badge will be issued. This should communicate to trainees that they may be scheduled on shifts and are expected to know all store operations.

Review and Repeat
- Make sure employees understand everything that was covered during the previous four stages of training, and ask for any questions.
- Have employees complete all Stage One cleaning procedures.

Sales Training Part V: Closing with an Add-On
- Explain to employees that during every transaction they should suggest an item to customers that complements their purchase.
- Make it clear that they should never ask, "Anything else?" That is usually answered with "No," which eliminates any chance of securing an add-on.
- After the customer decides upon the main item, convey the need for your sales team to be "painting a picture." For example, "Have you ever purchased a gift, gotten home, and realized it took a specific battery you didn't have? We have the right ones right over here."
- Explain that it's great when an employee suggests an item that she genuinely likes to a customer, because it is honest. When a staff member is genuine about her preferences, the customer is more likely accept the suggestion. For example, if you own a restaurant, have trainees try all of your desserts to decide upon their favorite. Then have them describe it to you so well that you can see it with your eyes closed.
- Make sure that employees understand that they only need to suggest one thing. We do not want to annoy a customer by suggesting a laundry list of items.

Register Training

♦ Train all parts of ringing up a sale including returns, mark-downs, and gift cards. Detail all procedures here.

Five Parts to a Sale Review

Have employees do each of the following:

♦ Demonstrate an appropriate greeting.
♦ Explain opening a Window of Contact, complete with an example they've constructed.
♦ Tell you what the one question we always ask a customer is.
♦ Explain the difference between a feature and benefit (features start with "it has." Benefits start with "so you.") Have them give you an example with a product you choose.
♦ Give you an example of an add-on.

If the trainees pass successfully, trade yellow In Training badges for green. Take them to the schedule and confirm their next shifts are closing shifts.

Stage Six Training

Again, provide an overview of the day's training. Explain that this final stage is mostly dedicated to learning to close the store as well as finer points of operation. After this training stage, employees are eligible for an evaluation and, potentially, a raise. The manager often handles this training stage to assess how well the new employees were trained and fit into the team.

Review and Repeat

♦ Make sure employees understand everything that was covered during the previous stage of training; ask if there are any questions.
♦ Have new employees complete all Stage One cleaning procedures.

Sales Training: Role Play

The specifics of this process are up to you but should always include the following:

- Build on Windows of Contact training during a conversation with your trainee.
- Explain how Windows of Contact can also be things you hear.
- Remember that the Windows of Contact goal is to share details—not just agree with someone. "I did that, too," will not stand out in a customer's mind when he leaves.
- Ask the trainees to present the features and benefits of one of your highest priced items.
- Pick up four items, take them to the register for trainees to ring up, and pay with gift card.
- Include information you had nowhere else to share here.

Register Training
- Role-play at the register using Windows of Contact, features and benefits, and add-ons.

Closing List
- Everyone must know how to close the store, even if the staff only works opening shifts.
- Show and explain thoroughly every item on the closing list.

It's also appropriate at this time to explain the probationary period and provide a written evaluation (or whatever you choose) to complete and certify employees as trained.

Trial Run

When you take a new employee through your training, remember that your goal is to be as thorough as possible—and ideally, to never have to repeat the training. If you scratch your head and wonder, "What did I mean by this?" then include more detail about it in your notes. For example, it's important to make it clear how often you expect something to be cleaned and exactly how you define clean. Don't just say, "Clean this," when you're instructing an employee on tidying the floor. Explain, instead, that, "My definition of clean it is that there are no dust bunnies, pins, crumbs, or anything else on the floor; you'd almost be able to eat off it." That means there is no room for error when someone is told, "Please go clean the shelves."

Creating a training program will help inoculate you from a bad hire. This is why it's necessary to evaluate new employees—based on criteria you've created—to see if they're up to the challenge of working for you as you develop your training program. If all the trainer can say about the trainee at the conclusion of training is, "He's nice"—be aware that this might not be the person to drive sales for your business.

Training the Four Personalities

When I was still a buck-toothed first grader with a bowl haircut, I was given a craft project that involved cutting out construction paper in the form of a giant key and inscribing it with the golden rule: "Do unto others as you would have others do unto you." Since that time, I strived—as I'm sure you have—to live my life by that maxim. But treating others, as you would yourself in this instance, would mean you could have a Driver training the way he wants to be trained: short, sweet, to the point, with a chance to quickly role-play. This is a potential disaster for an Amiable trainee who needs time to model herself after others, a chance to interact with a partner—and with *lots* of encouragement.

Do unto Others as They Want Done unto Themselves

Irish playwright George Bernard Shaw said it best: "Do not do unto others as you would expect they should do unto you. Their tastes may not be the same."

That's the key to understanding the four personalities—especially when training—you need to do unto others as *they* want done unto themselves.

When a Driver is being trained, he wants to know what to do to win the contest, get a raise, or secure a promotion, so structure your training like hoops through which they can jump. Natural fixers, Drivers may point out areas of improvement. They have to see how their positive results will get them more hours. Because Drivers are the most aggressive of the four personalities, many people don't even interview them, much less hire them. This is a shame, because while these individuals demand a lot, they give a lot as well. Even if they honestly tell you they will only be there six months, it may be worth it to train them, because they can be the quickest study—and the most driven.

Analyticals will pose a lot of "how" questions during training. Because they're process-oriented, they need an orderly progression through each and every step. Analyticals inherently try to make sense of whatever they hear, so watch their faces, as you explain things, for clues that they don't follow or agree with you. Think slow, steady, and methodical when presenting new information; you have to connect the dots. For example, if you're an Expressive trainer, you'll need to make sure you stay logically focused, whereas a Driver will have to tone down her natural hurry-up approach.

You'll probably be pulled in many directions when training Expressive personalities. They tend to ask questions the moment that they think of something, which may or may not be what you're covering at that time. Use patience in dealing with them and be sure to encourage their success. These are the spark plugs of your store, so don't clamp down on them. Encourage and appreciate their energy by making sure you train with excitement as well. Expressives hate to have someone be a downer. They often find Drivers to be demeaning, since these personality types correct without considering others' emotions; so be sure to ask how they are feeling as you train. Keep in mind as well that Expressives can have a bit of the con artist in them, so they may say they understand when they don't. Make sure to role-play or have them perform a task to your standards; they need to know the boundaries of a job so they can shine and avoid getting into trouble unknowingly.

Amiables tend *not* to ask questions when they don't understand something, so be sure to check them often to make training safe. Understand that Amiables can appear shy at first, so use Windows of

Contact to find things in common. Make it easy for them to make friends on the crew by introducing them and pointing out something they may have in common with another person. For example, "Karen, this is Tom; he's just starting with us today. I thought you two might get along because you both like Tom Petty and live in the Turtle Creek development." Don't leave Amiables alone with another employee without a checklist or they may just chat behind the counter. Without supervision, Amiables can seem the laziest of the bunch—they must have clear directions at all times. Because they're both Feelers, Expressives can naturally bring Amiables out of their shell, so consider pairing them together for training.

Once you get a sense of how each of the four personality types meets your business's demands, you'll be able to predict how they might handle certain situations. For example, if a customer tries to return something outside of the stated return policies, Drivers will get mad; they'll see someone trying to get away with something. In their eyes, it is a justice issue: right versus wrong. I once read about a hardware store manager who told a story about a guy trying to return four-year-old Westinghouse light bulbs. As an Analytical, he wondered, "How could someone do such a thing?" Like a Driver, an Analytical will instinctively stick on a policy and provide no middle ground.

Because they're the most independent, Expressives will tend to want to solve the problem, let the customer return the item without asking the manager—and then find a way to get around the fact they violated policy. An Amiable will call a manager to help the person rather than be put upon and have to deal with the conflict himself. You don't want this personality at your returns counter after the holidays, or you'll have a line of unhappy people waiting out the door.

Being aware of how these types react in certain situations will help you choose who should have additional responsibilities and who should not. To make sure your trainers know what is expected and use the training tools you have created, have them read the following section on how to train as well.

Train the Trainer

Most of us live with a critical parent inside our heads who got there as a result of all those well-meaning questions: "Did you wash your hands?" "Did you look both ways before you crossed the street?" Those questions resulted in well-meaning follow-up statements: "Your hands are not clean, and you have dirt under your nails." "You didn't look to the right, you could have been killed." Unfortunately, that critical parent is the voice we usually train with. You did this, and this, and this all wrong. *Who wants to work for someone like that?*

Like any parent or teacher knows, saying "don't" to someone creates a hole. Instead, you should tell trainees what to do to *replace* that behavior if you want them to act appropriately.

To combat criticism, convey it between statements about what they did right. Visualize this in terms of an Oreo cookie; in fact, go get yourself a package of them. (Yeah, I know they are supposed to be terrible for your body due to all the calories and fat, but you aren't going to eat them. Well, not in doing this exercise.)

An Oreo is a visual representation of the way many of us talk to our employees. We begin with a hard statement: "You did that wrong." Next a soft statement: "But you smiled during the greeting." And we end with another hard statement: "You forgot to do this again; I'm cutting your hours." *Again, who wants to be trained by someone like that?*

Grab one of the Oreos and twist it apart. Put the two solid cookie parts together, so the creamy white filling is on the top and bottom. That is how we need to talk to our employees—*especially* Feelers. Soft statement: "You really greeted the customer well with a smile." Hard statement: "You froze when you got to Windows of Contact, even though he had a Beatles album cover on the front of his shirt." Soft statement, "I know you love the Beatles; you could have had a conversation about it. Let's role-play it."

This is a great device with which to train your trainers as well. If someone is coaching incorrectly, you can simply ask, "Which type of Oreo was that?" Then if she gets the answer right—which she will— give her an Oreo.

THE TRAINER'S ROLE

Trainees must feel they are learning something throughout the day, so always encourage trainers to keep the following in mind:

1. What do I want my trainee to learn?
   a. Review the job description with the employee.
   b. Review each stage of training the day before, so you as a trainer are prepared.
   c. Review tasks at places like the register, where what the trainer or other employees have been doing may vary from the written training program. Perform each step fully prior to training.
   d. Give ample time to practice and ask questions before moving on.
   e. Don't spend more than 20 minutes instructing someone without a break. Come back to the task if necessary. After explaining something and practicing it, have the trainee do something menial to provide a mental break. Something that feels like drudgery to you will inevitably rub off on the trainee.
   f. Try to develop the ability to see what needs to be done, for example, the floor needs cleaning, that guy is waiting to be rung up, that woman is waiting for an answer to her question, and so forth. This way, trainers can be independent and still work productively instead of having to wait until an issue comes up.
2. When should the training be conducted?
   a. Schedule the trainer to work with the trainee during the slow times of the day and week when neither is required to actually interact with customers, otherwise the trainer will be distracted and the trainee won't get her full attention.
   b. Set a definite length of time for the training session—such as two- to three-hour maximum—as allowed by your state labor laws.
   c. Prepare a week's schedule to give to the trainee on the first day.

3. Why should the trainee learn only one way?

    a. You only train black and white—never grey. If the trainee has any question about what to do "if," have him write those questions down to be answered later in the day. The Expressive and the Analytical, especially, must be clear on the *one way* to perform each function first, but they must also be aware that you respect their need for answers.

    b. Explain the reasoning behind your procedures—why it's done a particular way so this doesn't happen and this does happen—and why it benefits the employee to do it the right way.

    c. Explain why it is important for customers that employees act in a consistent manner.

4. Is there a way to motivate the employee to learn the task correctly?

    a. Show trainees exactly what's in it for them. For example, you don't want your coffeehouse's customers to pour excess coffee in the trash at the condiment counter, because the trash bags break due to the weight of the water and you get grungy coffee-garbage-water all over your feet. That happens when the cashier doesn't ask at the register, "Would you like me to leave room for cream?" If you can connect the dots between the procedures you want done and why it's in their best interest, your training will go much more smoothly.

    b. Provide encouragement. Be generous with praise. Catch them doing something right more often than wrong. Intervene by asking questions before they create a problem to make it as easy as possible for the trainees to meet with success.

    c. Provide positive feedback. Point out errors gently, and don't be a nag. Trainees must remain receptive to the information.

    d. Remind trainees of the next stage of their training and review the progress that they've made.

    e. Remember: People respond to positive comments in a positive way and vice versa. If a trainee gives a snide answer, consider what you may have said to elicit it. When new employees feel vulnerable, they'll often try to protect their self-image by catching the trainer on something. This is normal and should be a sign of a low comfort level, so back up and give them the space to succeed at something, even if it is from a prior stage. We want them to enjoy training, not hate it or their trainer.

Four Steps for the Trainer to Train Effectively

1. **Tell:** Give an overview of what you are about to teach. Setting clear and specific goals and schedules is vital in encouraging the employee's success.

2. **Show:** After talking through the task, show the employee how to do it. Demonstrations help trainees understand how the components all fit together and into the rest of the job as well. Instruct slowly, and encourage questions.

3. **Do:** Have the employee do the task once you have demonstrated it. Watch and help, but stop the trainee if something is incorrect. Give honest, empathic feedback, and remember the importance of enhancing self-esteem. The task is easy for you because you've worked around your products for a long time; for the trainee, it is a lot of information in a short amount of time.

4. **Review:** Be sure to follow up by asking trainees questions about the task to make sure they fully understand. Make sure employees know how to spot situations that are out of the ordinary and coach them on how to handle those. ("What if . . . happened?" Questions are good.) Ask trainees for a commitment to do what you have asked; give encouragement and let them know you have confidence in their ability to do the task. Finally, ask them to tell you how to do the task.

Do, Don't Just Tell

An employee who is just starting is the most impressionable and can absorb the most information.

> ***Employees remember:***
> ◆ 10% of what they hear.
> ◆ 50% of what they see.
> ◆ 90% of what they do.

Six Stages of Training Overview for Trainers

STAGE ONE

This is a cleaning/stocking/paperwork stage during which trainees are given nametags and red In Training badges. The badge's color signifies that the trainee should not to be asked to perform additional duties by anyone other than the trainer, based on the written training program for that stage. While it's not likely to be a comfortable stage, if trainees can't or won't do those chores, they will never take responsibility for keeping your store clean and neat.

STAGE TWO

During this stage, trainees will learn about some additional operations of the store—including sales—and will be given a training packet and an assignment to learn before their next training stage begins.

STAGE THREE

This stage starts with a pretest and follows with training. Upon completion, trainees are issued yellow In Training badges, which lets others know to proceed with caution when asking the trainee to perform other tasks. Trainees are again assigned a section of the training packet to study.

STAGE FOUR

This stage begins with a product test, followed with training and another quiz to see what trainees have learned.

STAGE FIVE

This stage is dedicated to register training and customer service review. Once trainees pass the test for this stage, they get green In

Training badges. This will communicate that trainees may be scheduled on shifts and are expected to know all store operations.

STAGE SIX

This stage is dedicated to learning to close the store and the finer points of store operation. This completes the training; and at this point, trainees are eligible for an evaluation and/or a raise.

Final note to trainers: While there are no stupid questions, we do not want to keep repeating ourselves. Train for comprehension, not to get through a checklist. It is okay to dismiss a trainee during one of the six stages if the trainer feels that the trainee is not getting it, unable to learn, or not taking the training seriously.

Oh—and if you're wondering how Jane Lindley got even after finding out it was I who turned on the sprinklers? She TPed my house during a rainstorm. Now *that* was mean.

STAT: *Five Things to Do Immediately after Reading This Chapter*

1. Examine your employee training program to see what's missing.
2. Craft a script for how you want employees to engage customers on the phone.
3. Develop a detailed six-stage plan to train a new hire.
4. Create the necessary checklists and forms requiring employee signatures.
5. Decide who will do your training. Set up a certification on your new system that proves that trainers know what is expected and how a well-trained employee will perform.

Chapter 6

Building and Coaching Your Team

If you damage the cells of a vital organ such as your lungs by engaging in harmful behavior, like smoking two packs of cigarettes a day, you can end up with emphysema—or worse. The same kind of situation can occur if you allow bad employees to linger; you might end up with a store at which no one wants to shop. One bad apple can indeed spoil the barrel.

This chapter's goal is to show you how to make all the individuals you've hired and trained into a cohesive sales team. Building a team that is focused on selling requires your commitment to hiring only the best, having a detailed training program, giving clear expectations with boundaries, and rewarding excellent performance.

What do you want your sales team to do? In short, they move product. It doesn't matter if they're nice people, really need the job, or happen to be relatives; it doesn't matter if you would want to have them over for holiday dinner. The only thing that matters is: Are they able to help you grow your business and improve the financials we discussed in Chapter 1? They need to be focused on the customer and adding value—not stocking shelves and finding something to keep busy—when they are on your sales floor.

This chapter helps you set expectations and boundaries for all four employee personalities. It demonstrates how you can show them the rewards of working for your business, and, if necessary, the door.

Set the Bar and the Guardrails

You must set an expectation from the beginning that your new employee has to comprehend immediately: your definition of work. The work—or the bar for which employees are to reach—is to make a customer feel at that very moment that they are the most important person in the world. Just for those few minutes, their cares are your employees' cares. If your employees don't understand this, you need to let them know that your store may not be a good fit for them.

Be a Chameleon

When you can manage each of the four personality types to meet their needs, you'll have lower turnover and a diverse crew that works well together. You must change your approach like a chameleon changes its skin color to match each personality's working style if you want to get the most out of your employees. To recap:

There are two main types of personalities, those ruled by their head (Thinkers), and those ruled by their heart (Feelers). If you run your business without objective employee reviews, formal training programs, or criteria for performance, you probably are a Feeler—either an Expressive or an Amiable. The Expressive personalities want to know *who* is going to be there and express their opinions freely. The Amiables—the largest segment of the population—want to know *why* and are driven by wanting to be likeable (or amiable) and part of the group.

If, on the other hand, you have a handbook chock-full of policies, procedures, and punishments, you're probably a Thinker—either a Driver or an Analytical. Drivers want to know *what*; they are *driven* by results and status. Analyticals want to know *how* something works and prefer to *analyze* results and outcomes. While Drivers want to just get the job done, Analyticals want to get the job done the right way. Expressives want to do a job *their* way, and Amiables want to know who else will do the job *with* them. Drivers are happy *doing*; Analyticals are happy *thinking*; Expressives are happy *playing*; and Amiables are happy *listening*.

Just knowing this information about each personality type can help you figure out how to talk to them. But what if you are an Analytical who's managing an opposite personality like an Expressive? Look to the shortcomings of your personality type for clues as to what can create friction.

Helping Drivers Get Results

Drivers (like me) tend to talk fast, want people to get to the point, and steamroll our thoughts over others. If this explanation sounds like you, being aware of your habits should help you slow down in both the speed with which you speak and your expectation for others to "get it." Drivers tend to cut to the chase, while Feelers need to see the whole journey with lots of details. It's important for Drivers to learn to encourage others' opinions and thoughts before laying down the law and stating that "this is what we're going to do." The things that make you successful are the very things that can trip you up. One personality profile equates the Driver to the eagle.

When you manage Drivers, you need to assure them that they are your equal before they'll take your advice. They're so confident in what they know and want that it takes some serious effort to convince them otherwise. Drivers also fear being last in sales or standings, so reinforce them whem they are number one. And if they're number two, show them how easy it would be to get to first place. If you don't get this right, Drivers will be the first to leave you looking for someone who will appreciate them. Want to kill a Driver? Ignore him, take credit for his idea, or patronize him.

Showing Analyticals a Process

Analytical personalities tend to come off as detached, cold, and aloof; they're only interested the bottom line. In the classic Aesop's Fable *The Ant and the Grasshopper*, the ant is an Analytical because he's always prepared. This can be taken too far, though, in terms of overthinking or overplanning, which can result in making no decisions. If you're an Analytical, find a way to become excited about a product, a meeting, a new day. I find that many business owners are unaware of how their Analytical personalities come across to their crews until it is too late. That's why some liken this personality type to the owl. So force yourself to smile and offer encouragement in words that people—especially Feelers—need to hear; think *great*, not adequate.

You must make it clear to any Analyticals that you manage that you see things in their logical way; because unlike Expressives, they see a clear beginning, middle, and end to projects. Try to show them that your way is more efficient than some others. Because Analyticals are afraid of missing something, take your time. Accept the fact that this group may not participate in all your joking and banter—something that can make them seem aloof. Want to kill an Analytical? Tell her to lighten up or not be such a perfectionist.

Helping Expressives Focus

Expressives tend to be extroverts who often make their private business public, sharing information without boundaries. An opposite of the Analytical, the Expressive is Aesop's grasshopper, living for today. Expressives worry about being like everybody else instead of being recognized for their uniqueness. Again, their enthusiasm and energy are the spark plugs for your team. Their showiness can be compared to that of a peacock.

If this is your personality type, try to listen more carefully and set specific, realistic goals, since your enthusiasm can make you feel a bit invincible at times and can overwhelm Analyticals who want "just the facts." "Keep your eyes on the prize" is a good motto for managing others if you are an Expressive.

If, however, you are managing Expressives, remember that they have to process externally while Thinkers don't. Answer Expressives' questions as they happen or request that they write them down to be answered later the same day. If you don't, they will become impatient with you for dismissing their concerns. Expressives are the first not to show up because they found something else to do—and might lie about it.

Want to kill an Expressive? Because this personality tends to wear its heart on its sleeve, cynicism cuts like a knife and can even result in tears. Tread lightly when it comes to their emotions.

Making Amiables Your Friend

Amiables are very malleable and rarely take a stand. Their easygoing style can allow for sloppiness; and their desire to be everyone's friend can cloud their perception of change and professional standards. They are, by nature, the peacemakers, which is why some equate them to the dove. If you're an Amiable, then it's best to write out your goals and the follow-up steps that are necessary to achieve them. Edit yourself to the *point* of the story, not all the extraneous details that lead up to it. Speed up your interactions with customers and employees to fight your natural inclination to relax and get to know people. Firing is especially hard for Amiable owners, because they feel they personally failed in getting someone to fully participate on their team. If that's you, order an employee's final check well in advance of a final meeting to make sure you follow through and remove the nonperformer.

If you are managing an Amiable, remember that these people love stories, which works well because stories tend to stick in all of our minds as pictures. You need to befriend these employees, because they often fear not being liked. Windows of Contact is the tool to use with them. Amiables are most comfortable avoiding confrontation. Well-meaning supervisors try to manage them by being nice and sparing their feelings, but that is the worst way to supervise these employees. Amiables believe that the world (you included) is basically going to be understanding, which makes it tough to manage them—especially if you are an Amiable as well. They are the ones who will *never* quit, so, if you don't give them direction or feedback, they will assume everything is okay. Want to kill an Amiable? Be impatient with him for not working fast enough.

Managing for 2010 and beyond is more about personality type and positive mind-set than a strict set of how-tos. Business owners must rethink their belief that they can control others and change *their* behavior while ignoring their own. Speaking all four languages as needed helps you get the most out of your sales team.

Motivating Employees

A woman once asked me during a seminar, "How can we motivate our employees to do their jobs?" I offhandedly answered, "The truth is no one can motivate another person. You can hold a carrot, but it will only work if the person wants that carrot. Motivation to want to do a good job must come from within." She sat with arms crossed, obviously upset with my answer; she was looking for a way to make her employees work.

I continued, "A good employee has to have the drive to do the right thing, even when you're not there watching everything." A great employee finds tasks to complete, exceeds expectations, and makes the manager look good. Too often, we find people who are not self-directed, friendly, or ready to work in retail, but we hire them anyway. These people really don't like retail to begin with, but we scratch our heads trying to come up with bonuses, contests, and rewards to get them do to the minimum requirements of the job.

This is the wrong approach. You shouldn't have to find ways to get your employees to do the basics—no matter what personality type they are. The rewards come when they *exceed* expectations; adding on to every sale, driving average check, and increasing average number of items in a sale are the things that should get them a bonus. Better job done equals more hours and potential raises. I suppose then, in that sense, you *can* motivate them to exceed minimum job requirements.

But doing a cleaning checklist? No. Following an hourly bake schedule? No way. Arriving on time to work? Nope. A manager has to make tough calls, the most basic of which is hiring a good crew and, if necessary, saying to one of them: "You're not cutting it." People cannot wait for you to motivate them to change; they have to motivate themselves to do the job for which they were hired.

While I'm all about giving people a chance, it's up to them to provide results for the money you pay them—not act like charity cases who require you to look the other way. "Bless her heart, she's trying," is fine for a grandma to say but not a boss. And while I'm at it: If you use volunteers to run your gift shop, nonprofit, or other business, you have to hold them as accountable as an employee. Don't settle for subpar or you'll be gone.

Can you motivate someone? Yes. Just tell your employees, "This is what the job requires," and if they can't motivate themselves, "My way or the highway." You're the boss.

Now you have an idea of why it's necessary to be a chameleon in terms of dealing with your employees' various personalities in specific ways. How, then, do you make them into a team? You do it through regular reinforcement of high sales expectations.

Regular Store Meetings Are Key

Your crew's attitude about selling will affect the altitude of your sales. You must counter the gloom-and-doom mentality of the morning news, or your employees will bring this outlook into your business and onto your sales floor. Who will do this for your staff if not you? You can build a positive culture of sales with your crew one morning a week, an hour before your store opens. Use the following steps to create your agenda.

1. **Welcome everyone.** If someone is new, introduce him and everyone else. It's always fun if you ask the new employee to tell everyone his favorite movie and why; then let others share theirs.

2. **Review sales for the month.** How's everything going on this front? Emphasize progress and find something to be positive about, even if sales are off. Is the average number of units per sale going up? Did you see an increase in one category during the past week? The purpose of store meetings is to lift spirits, not dampen them. Don't *lie*, of course, but don't paint with a red brush if things aren't going as well as you'd hoped.

3. **Deal with policies and procedures.** Has anything new come up? Did you deal with any problems over the past week like tardiness, employee discounts, or covering shifts that you want to address? This is the time and place to deal with it.

4. **Boost product knowledge.** Take one product and teach its features and benefits. It could be a new item or one that's particularly high profit. This is a good time to ask if your staff has questions about the product or its use. Employees would get bonus points if they can try it on, put it together, or use it in some fashion.

5. **Discuss contests and prizes.** Provide updates on a current one, announce a new one, or reward a past one.

6. **Share inspirational sales stories.** Share complimentary customer service letters as well as stories from sales books like *The Retail Doctor's*® *Guide To Growing Your Business, Think and Grow Rich* (Napoleon Hill, 2005), or *See You at the Top* (Zig Ziglar, 2000). Ask employees if they have any encouraging stories to share.

7. **Try role-playing.** See who can create the biggest sale, overcome objections to price using features and benefits, and so on.

8. **Hold a round-robin.** Go around the room and have each employee participate in some way, through feedback or questions. This will help to make sure they were paying attention.

Following the agenda in this order helps your crew remain aware of your expectations. Never try to ad-lib a meeting; if it's important enough to pay your employees to come in, then it's absolutely necessary for you to plan out those 30 minutes. Make sure that you arrive early so you have plenty of time to arrange, set up props, and put out a box of doughnuts or other treats; then simply follow your agenda.

I discourage the idea of holding staff meetings after work. Employees won't be able to spend their day putting what you've discussed into practice. They're also likely to be tired and/or constantly checking their watches with one foot out the door. You want them to be fully engaged for these sessions.

Beware of the personality of the employee who wants to trap you—a phenomenon that I call, "kill the leader." Anytime one person is in front of a group, there is a natural tendency to find fault with that individual. That's why so few people want to speak in public; they're afraid of the audience member who will try to shoot down their ideas. This person might start with an innocent, "Well, what if . . . ?" and may continue to try to catch you—especially if you show that you're unsure or uncomfortable. It could be about a policy or procedure or something that you addressed during a role-play. Oftentimes, this is an Expressive personality at work, seeking attention and wanting her needs to be met or a Thinker showing how smart they are by showing the leader up. Don't let them! You never want to let a meeting devolve into a bitching or griping session, so make sure you thoroughly understand what someone could say to derail you, and table any issues that you don't feel comfortable defending at the moment.

Toward the last 10 minutes of your meeting, devise a contest that pits two groups of employees against each other. I worked with Creative Kidstuff, a toy store in Minneapolis, Minnesota, where we split the group into two teams to see which could build the biggest add-on sale. Each team invented a sales scenario and then ran around the store selecting items that its fictional customer would buy. At the end of five minutes, both teams had a pile of games, toys, and accessories and an explanation of why they chose what they did. Performing this exercise improved their sales skills. They had fun doing it, and made great connections like pairing the book *Good Night Moon* (Margaret Wise Brown and Clement Hurd, Harper Collins, 1991) with the glow-in-the-dark stars. This ultimately led them to think about add-ons more often and with seemingly unrelated items that worked well together.

Finish each meeting with a round-robin by going around the room asking each person, "What's one thing you learned today?" or "What did we talk about today?" You want to be sure everyone was actively listening and contributes something. If there's someone who can't seem to give any feedback, ask him a question to encourage his success. If that doesn't work, speak privately with the individual afterward to find out what was going on.

Senior employees who have been with you a year or more—and who have heard most of your stuff already—should share responsibility for running these meetings to grow their own leadership skills. Be sure to have them present to you prior to the meeting so you can coach anything that is unclear.

For a quick meeting to set good expectations for the day—especially during the holidays—my friend and speaker Ian Percy shared this suggestion: "Many salespeople come to work thinking that life sucks and customers are cheap, demanding, and ignorant; and their beliefs are confirmed. The universe gives us what we think about; we create the very things we fear, and our wounds are usually self-inflicted. So take five minutes every morning before the doors open to have everyone meet and discuss wonderful expectations for the day—how terrific customers eager to buy will soon enter the store and what a privilege it will be to serve them. Just five minutes is all it takes to tell the universe what kind of day you'd like to have."

Now what was your honest reaction as you read that suggestion? Ninety-eight percent of readers will have had a negative reaction: "That's stupid and naive." "Staff won't show up five minutes early." "What a waste of time." Well, guess what? If that's what you think, then you'll be right.

We've got to get back to believing that we can change and do better. You can only grow a sales team if you are willing to raise and monitor your expectations, hold your staff accountable, and perform the uncomfortable job of correcting their behavior.

Employee Reviews

Using regular employee reviews and written warnings enables you to constantly prune your bottom 20 percent—your lowest performing employees—to grow your business. Because of that, you should *never stop hiring.*

There was a famous experiment at a Western Electric plant in Cicero, Illinois, during the 1920s, when researchers attempted to discover the best illumination for worker productivity. They first checked the productivity of the regular factory to establish a baseline. Next, they told the crew they were going to increase some of the lights, and worker productivity picked up. They added more lights and productivity continued to grow. And although the researchers neglected to turn on the extra lights during the final stage, worker productivity *still* increased. These experiments led to what is now called "The Hawthorne Effect"—which means that people change their performance in response to *any* increase in attention paid to them.

That's precisely why it is so important to stay engaged with your employees, monitor their progress, and find as many ways as possible for your best people to shine. Conducting employee reviews is a necessary element of this. You should complete one 30 days after you've hired a new employee, 90 days after that, and then once every 6 months. It's easy to schedule these; just set them up automatically in whatever e-mail calendar system you and your staff use.

Employee reviews make you aware of the things that make an employee a *good* employee. They let you give feedback on your concerns, hear theirs, and yes, sometimes reward them with a raise or deliver a reprimand.

Think of an employee review as a chance to get together with your staff members around a set of questions. You don't want them to expect that they will necessarily receive a raise each time or that something bad is about to happen; a review is just part of your process. (You can see an example of an employee review online, details in the back of this book.)

Creating a Goal Sheet

You need to have a storewide sales goal that is set before the start of each new month and that is easy for your crew to see. It could be based on last year's number times a percentage increase or on the past two months' business. It could be a variation of the two, but it must be reasonable and doable. I recently took a call from a guy who expected his crew to achieve a 30 percent increase from the previous year. "Why?" I asked. "Because that's what I need."

A goal cannot be some dreamed up figure that the business has no history of achieving. Otherwise, it is very defeating for the employees, especially Drivers; and you will actually *demotivate* them.

Once you've developed your realistic goal, break it down into what you need to do each week; make adjustments for busier versus slower days. Your employees also need to know how much they personally have to do to meet their commission or bonus goals. So before the month starts, figure out how many hours each person will work, total them up, and divide the store goal by your total crew hours.

Employees	# Hours Expected to Work this Month	Projected Goal	105%
Joe	160	10,076	10,580
Joan	120	7,557	7,935
Jimmy	100	6,297	6,612
Jane	100	6,297	6,612
Jeff	80	5,038	5,290
Jazar	60	3,778	3,967
Total Projected Employee Hours	560		
Store Goal	35,265		
Avg per Hour per Employee	62.97		
Total of Employees Goals			40,996

FIGURE **6.1**   Storewide Sales Goals

The result is an average amount per hour that each employee needs to sell to achieve the goal. To allow for schedule changes, multiply that by 105 percent, then multiply that by each person's expected monthly hours, and you'll have his or her expected monthly goal. You can give them an accurate goal once the final week schedule is confirmed and everyone's hours are refactored.

To create a visual reminder of each employee's goal and the store goal, create a daily goal sheet like the one pictured in Figure 6.2 on the following page. First thing every morning, take a yellow pad of paper and make columns across the top with every salesperson's name who will be working that day. Write the store goal in the right-hand margin; below it, divide the daily goal into 30-minute segments. If, for example, you knew you needed to do $3,000 one day, and you were open 11 hours, you'd divide the $3,000 by 22 half-hour segments to see that you should be at $136 by 10:30 A.M. In the columns to the left, enter the names of employees who will work that day. Write a daily goal above that by multiplying the number of hours the person is scheduled to work by your hourly average for that month. You could also do this in a program like Excel. Place the sheet on a clipboard next to the register.

BOB: $1,000	DAVID $800	JERI: $600	TER: $600	VICKI: $300	STORE GOAL: 3,128	2/1/01	Reading
45	296	545		35			
100	39	34		109	136	at 10:30 ✓	
$145	335	579		244	272	at 11 ✓	
697	79				408	at 11:30 ✓	
842	414				544	at Noon ✓	$690
					680	at 12:30 ✓	
					816	at 1	
					952	at 1:30	
					1,088	at 2	
					1,224	2:30	
					1,360	at 3	
					1,496	at 3:30	$725
					1,632	at 4	$2,079
					1,768	at 4:30	
					1,904	at 5	
					2,040	at 5:30	
					2,176	at 6	
					2,312	at 6:30	
					2,448	at 7	
					2,584	at 7:30	
					2,720	at 8	
					2,856	at 8:30	
					3,000	at 9	

FIGURE 6.2   Sales as Recorded by Hand on Legal Pad

Instruct employees to record totals under their names on the sheet after ringing up a sale and to keep a running total as they add to it. While your register can keep track of this amount, it makes a more significant impact when it's written down; this way, everyone can see who's selling what at any time; very important to Drivers and Expressives.

Match your register readings to the goal on the right of the sheet several times during the day, and check off the sales you've achieved so far.

In the example shown in Figure 6.2, you can see that the crew had already hit 12:30 P.M.'s goal by noon. And while employees weren't on pace to hit their 4 P.M. goal, it looks like a 3:30 rush hit. Suddenly, they could all see that they were again on track to make the daily goal.

For particularly high-volume periods during the holidays, break the especially high goals into smaller (as little as 15-minute) segments to make each one more manageable. Inch by inch, goal making's a cinch.

The kind of people you've hired and the training you've given them should result in a group that is eager to compete. Each salesperson wants to know that he is the best at what he does; so give them all ways to do just that.

Shark Charts

You can create your own Shark Charts to maintain a visual representation of both store and employee goals. Shark Charts helps you highlight your top salespeople and motivate the others, and they are easy to create using graph paper or again on your computer with Excel.

As seen in Figure 6.3, you simply write out the days of the month across the bottom and ascending numbers in units of two or three dollars on the left side. Take the store's monthly goal divided by the number of

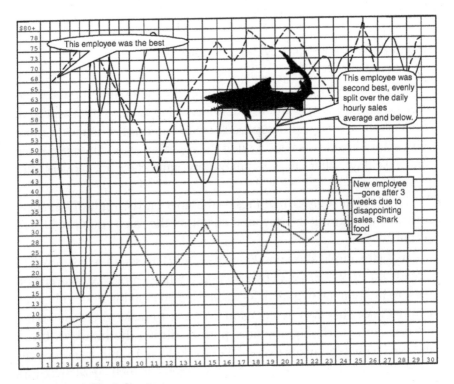

FIGURE 6.3   A Shark Chart

hours you are open, and draw a heavy line at the corresponding dollar value about three-quarters of the way up from the bottom. About midway on that line, draw a big fin coming out of the water.

For the employee Shark Chart, add a legend that represents each staff member with a different color. Take the previously determined average dollar per hour that all salespeople have to sell, and draw a heavy line at the corresponding dollar value (also about three-quarters of the way up from the bottom with a fin). At the end of each day, take your store sales and place a dot for that day on your store's Shark Chart; connect the dots daily. Take each employee's total sales on the second Shark Chart and divide them by the number of hours each person worked; this will equal the employee's sales per hour. Place a corresponding dot each day on your employee Shark Chart as well. Connecting the dots here will make it obvious who is doing the job and who isn't. Another alternative is to do a Shark Chart for number of items per unit sale.

Post both charts in a spot where every employee can see them daily (perhaps by the timecards if you still use them, a lunchroom, or break room). If it becomes clear that a given employee is underwater much of the time, take him aside and explain that he must get his sales above water. Offer to work with the employee on an individual basis. But if he can't cut it, like human shark bait—he must be gone quickly.

Tracking these kinds of numbers show your employees that you are watching them, and the best will crow about their accomplishments. If you ignore such numbers, employees get bored, customer service issues arise, and people quit because they don't feel appreciated or valued (especially Driver and Expressive personalities).

In addition to using employee reviews to evaluate performance, you want to find out how well employees go out of their way to create an exceptional experience for first-time customers. And that's why you need to use mystery shops.

Mystery Shoppers

A mystery shopper is someone who poses as a normal customer purchasing a product, asking questions, or behaving in a certain, predetermined way—and who then provides a report to the business owner about her experiences. The results of a mystery shop provide a snapshot of a moment in time. A mediocre employee can receive a one-time score of 90 percent, while one of your better employees could get a 70 percent on an off day. That's precisely why you need a series of regular shops over a period of time. When you have three, four, or five mystery shoppers in one month who all report the same (hopefully positive!) result, you've established a pattern. This becomes a scorecard for your training program—your standards and employees' performance from a customer's point of view. Don't be complacent because you get lots of compliments from loyal customers. Mystery shops are to see how new customers experience your store; they are the ones most likely to move your financials upward.

Did you catch the coverage of President Obama's burger run to Five Guys Burgers in Washington, D.C., last year? One of the big reasons that the chain is doing so well is because it sends secret shoppers to all locations twice a week. Five Guys knows you need to inspect what you expect.

In order to achieve consistently high standards, you have to make sure that the right employees do the right things. Training new employees to 100 percent performance and then scheduling them under managers who don't run the shifts up to par spins your company's wheels—and lowers the brand perception in customers' eyes. It thereby destroys profits.

The number one thing business owners tell me is, "I just need more customers." *Wrong;* you need more customers to *return.* You can't attract everyone in a two-mile radius to try your store, deliver lousy results, and expect to get more bodies in the door. You can burn through a whole neighborhood with bad word-of-mouth, and without mystery shoppers, you may never know why.

Five Guys, with 436 franchisees, sees the value in conducting nearly 50,000 shops per year—so why shouldn't you? Oh, right—the money. Most retailers don't blink at spending $500 per month in advertising, yet they balk at spending a fraction of that to measure customer experience. That's just plain dumb. Profit comes from the people who want to tell their friends about you and return themselves, not from the discount promotions you offer to entice new shoppers. And please, drop the idea that mystery shops are a way to spy on employees for compliance; that's only what they'll think if you don't present it correctly. You certainly don't need a mystery shop to justify your desire to fire someone.

If you aren't servicing your customers the way they believe you should, you essentially invite competitors who are eager to take your business. It's not what your regulars tell you but what the *new* customers share that matters most.

Benefits of Mystery Shops

- Monitor and measure service performance.
- Improve customer retention.
- Make employees aware of what is important when serving customers.
- Monitor facility conditions.
- Ensure product or service delivery quality.
- Support promotional programs.
- Allow for competitive analyses between locations.
- Identify training needs and sales opportunities.
- Ensure positive customer relationships on the frontline.
- Enforce employee integrity and knowledge.
- Support hustle by employees to meet customers.

Not all mystery shopping companies are the same; far from it, in fact. One Fortune 500 CEO client of mine told me how he discovered that the shoppers he hired from a cheap shopping service had never even *been* to his store; you get what you pay for. Another said she'd tried it but that it "didn't work." It was obvious when I looked at her mystery shop form exactly *why* it wasn't successful; every single question was subjective. "Did you feel valued as a guest?" "Did they attempt to meet your needs?" "Did you feel welcomed?" Shoot me. These are terrible questions! What would feedback have looked like to the employee who got a low score on her shop? How would one even begin to measure these responses? "Gee, Sally, the customer didn't feel valued as a guest. Try harder." Reminds me of the old days in chorus when the conductor yelled at us to "sing in tune." If we knew *how* to do that, we would have done it.

Like your training procedures, questions on a mystery shop need to be black and white. For example:

◆ Did the server say, "Good morning, good afternoon, or good evening"?
◆ Did the salesperson describe an item using features (it has) with the benefits (so you can)?
◆ Were you invited to sign up for our e-mail club?

The mystery shop company I use has both a compliance black-and-white criteria as well as a narrative so compelling that you can actually *see* the transaction in the store. I work with clients to get their mystery shopper surveys done correctly and, therefore, produce action-able results. Because mystery shops gauge how well your sales process works, a good narrative shows how each personality type responds to your employees. Analytical or Driver shoppers might just want to know *will this work?* And to what degree? An Amiable shopper could be looking for someone to come over and help her, while an Expressive might remark about a salesperson, "She was so bright and bubbly." A well-constructed mystery shop lets you see how all four personalities' needs are met.

How to present mystery shop results to your crew? Meet one-on-one with the manager and go over the good and not so good using the Oreo method we discussed earlier. Encourage the manager to do the same with the employees, rewarding particularly good service. Never just post shop results on a bulletin board with a circled score. Those who didn't get evaluated will be relieved it wasn't them, snicker at those who did a poor job, and go on with their business. Mystery shops are a gift of reality to your training and managing programs.

One client of mine with 14 locations is now the top location in her franchise; another's average check rose 10 percent in three months. Is it a mystery? Nope; it's a mystery shop. To that end, I have a special offer for a great mystery shopping company at the back of this book.

In order to succeed as we emerge from the recent recession—and as competitors cry the blues and leave your market—you need to consistently provide clear expectations and demand high employee standards. After all, your customers deserve and pay for those.

Employee Recognition

It can be tough to come up with meaningful staff rewards. One approach is to ask employees what might motivate them to go out of their way to achieve a goal prior to beginning a contest. You can include a dollar amount for first, second, and third place. It might take a bit more effort to plan, but it makes the carrot you dangle more meaningful.

Contests can create problems due to differences between the four personality types. Driver or Expressive salespeople will do anything to make a sale. They might even resort to dishonest tactics like keeping information from customers, pulling off a sale tag before showing customers an item, or wheeling and dealing your prices—especially true if they are disgruntled.

I was reading the *Los Angeles Times* one Sunday in 1986 when I spotted an ad for a five-piece Lenox Autumn china setting for $48.88. Since my first paying job was to clean and polish the china and silver at Slavick's jewelry store—back when a place setting cost $125—I knew that this was an incredible deal. I didn't want china, but because it was such a great bargain, I called the South Coast Plaza Bullock's store to see if it carried that place setting at this price. The person who answered the phone said it was a typo, no dice. I called the Del Amo Fashion Center and asked if the price was correct. The salesperson, Bruce, told me he would make an exception and asked how many settings I wanted. I said six. He told me it would take a few months for delivery and that I'd save an additional 10 percent if I opened a credit account. I did and upped the order to eight. Over the next few months, Bruce called and offered yet another extra discount and told me that if I wanted, he'd re-ring that day so he could win a contest. I ended up with twelve five-piece place settings for somewhere around $30 each. As a customer, all the deals Bruce gave me were great, but this kind of extra-special discount treatment on the part of a particular salesperson can be deadly for a store owner.

You must make any contest as fair as possible to deal with the personality types who tend to look for loopholes. For instance, Amiables who don't think they can win may opt to help a colleague, because they care more about making friends than winning contests. Expressives or Drivers, the most competitive personalities, may feel the deck is stacked against them because of their schedule or limited number of hours. You can counteract this tendency by dividing total sales by number of hours each employee works to level the playing field, instead of running a contest only for total sales. A contest's purpose is to grow sales, not hinder employee motivation. Consider holding two contests, and pitting the morning against the evening shift for highest number of units per hour sold.

A final note about prizes: A check is the worst prize, because employees don't see the full amount once taxes are taken out. It's better to give cash in single-dollar bills or something else that makes a visual impression. Gift certificates are okay, but paid time off is better. The most effective prizes I've seen are memorable rewards—like trips or even furniture—that employees can tell their friends they won from you.

Recognition Isn't Always a Motivator

I saw the following post on the blog Evil HR Lady (http://evilhrlady.blogspot.com/2009/09/whats-in-it-for-me.html) from an HR director:

"I work in a small creative firm and have an employee who is technically very good, but . . . our company recently ran an internal contest to rewrite our phone system message to the outside world. The first thing this employee asked [about the contest] was, 'What's in it for me? Are there prizes or anything?' When the contest creator explained that the winner would get corporate recognition in the newsletter, this person responded that this wasn't enough. [He felt that] the company was 'saving money' by not hiring someone creative to do it, [and therefore] didn't feel 'incented' to participate. [As an HR director], I was [informed about his] 'attitude.' I'm looking for a nonconfrontational way to explain that this kind of attitude is going to hurt this person's career—here or anywhere—and encourage him to reconsider how he responds to these kinds of things. Can you help? [Or is it] unrealistic to think that I can somehow influence a person to change this kind of behavior?"

As one might expect, the blog prompted a variety of comments, including one from someone who said: "Games and contests are good motivators for some individuals and worthless to others. I don't do many games, either. To those of us who show up for the paycheck alone, that sort of thing is often meaningless. [This employee] may not have meant to be snarky, but simply [meant to express that he wasn't] interested. The game is not the type of motivation this individual needs."

Did you notice the two types of personalities clashing? The Amiable HR staff member is reluctant to confront the problem employee, yet wants to help him somehow. Meanwhile, the Analytical honestly assesses that the corporate recognition approach simply used the wrong motivation for this individual. This is a clear example of the amount of management time that you can save if you just make an effort to understand the four basic personalities before jumping to conclusions.

The Sales Equation

Salespeople know that they have to strike a balance between talking and listening, presenting the product and matching it to the customers' desires. They know they have to build trust before and not after the sale.

But not everyone you meet will want to buy from you. Some people really are just looking. That's why you need to understand and teach the formula for sales: SW, SW, SW, N; which stands for, "Some will. Some won't. So what? *Next!*

Being a salesperson is a lot like being a baseball pitcher; the more you pitch strikes, the more likely you are to duplicate them. The greats know that the only way to do better is practice how they approach the pitch. The sales process is the same kind of game: the more customers you meet, the better your skills become, and the more likely you are to close the sale on a regular basis.

However, it all starts with a genuine desire to meet people and move merchandise. Without both of these traits, the nicest guy in the world might never be able to sell because he talks so much. This irritates owners and customers alike. If, on the other hand, you're approached by a salesperson who only sees you as a sale to be made, you feel empty and used because he sold you something that you tell yourself later you didn't need.

The only way to build trust is to slow down and focus, silence your judgments, open your eyes, and see that there is an individual in front of you. Not a prospect. Not a guest. A *person*. Only when you afford yourself the luxury of making a connection before you try to move the merchandise will you have any hope of making a sale.

Yes, your sales employee can find out at the register that the customer's daughter goes to the same school as yours. But that's too late in the sales process to make a difference. Yes, he can share an amusing tale of putting together his own kid's bicycle for her birthday while the customer signs the credit card pad, but it doesn't matter at that point. Yes, he can follow up with a handwritten thank-you note the next day. But if he didn't establish trust at the beginning, it rings hollow and is a waste.

If your employee did all of those things right and the customer walked anyway, he—and you—just have to realize that you can't win them all. Remember: SW, SW, SW, N. Your goal is to lower the number of walks, analyze the reasons, and whenever possible, coach before they walk away so you can increase your conversion rates. Then hone your skills with the next person who walks in the door.

Raises and Promotions

I have a saying for any employee who asks for a pay increase: "Your raise becomes effective as soon as you do." The idea here is that employees deserve to be rewarded only *after* they have achieved success.

If your employees are eager to advance, let them know what they need to do to get more hours, a raise, or even their own store. Advancement should always be based on who is best able to sell your products; it doesn't just depend on who has been with you the longest—especially if you are looking to promote an Amiable. Do they have to hit goal three months in a row? Do they need to beat year-over-year for a quarter? The parameters are up to you, but more often than not, we simply never tell our employees what they are. That's when they (especially Drivers) look to your competitor for advancement and leave you in the lurch.

To let guests honor their servers, Atlanta's Baltimore Crab & Seafood Restaurant has a "Walk of Fame." On random nights, servers and chefs receive kudos via autographed golden stars—filled out anonymously by guests—to be used later by the restaurant for drawings among employees for quarterly incentive bonuses.

There are myriad ways of showing employees via rewards that we value them; one of the most time-honored is to give additional responsibilities and a raise. It's tempting to reward your most effective morning employee, by promoting her to assistant manager, and then have her work nights; thinking that since nights have been slow, she'll help improve business. However, this separates the employee from the colleagues and customers with whom they worked so well to make great sales in the morning. If she stays in that night position without the stimulus of store visitors, you often run into management issues that arise from attempting to shoehorn a valuable Feeler salesperson into a mediocre time slot.

When you promote, look at how the employee's personality meshes with the new position's responsibilities. Then have an honest, private talk with her prior to announcing the change in position to the rest of the staff.

How to Deal with Employees' "Survivor Guilt"

I received this e-mail the other day from Tricia Masing: "Bob, my staff is going through your Sales Rx: The Five Parts to a Successful Sale DVD training. During one of the store meetings, we discussed barriers, [and] one employee admitted that she sometimes feels guilty selling high-end items when she doesn't think the customer can afford it. Yikes! Another said that she could relate to that. GM laid off one employee's husband; another owned a store that closed a year ago; and we all have friends, neighbors and family facing financial hardship. [Their reaction] was unexpected because these are very friendly, social people, and I . . . expected them to breeze through the Five Parts to a Successful Sale process. I don't want my staff to feel guilty about helping customers buy high-end items; I don't want customers to feel guilty about spending; and I don't want anyone to feel guilty about us staying in business! Do you have any words of wisdom on how to slay the guilt monster?"

A note: This business owner was from Michigan, where the AP reported unemployment rates ranged from a low of 10 percent in Ann Arbor to a high of 17 percent in Flint. Of course people are scared.

Traditionally, "survivor guilt" is the term used to describe the feelings of those who emerge from a disaster that mortally engulfs others—like the sole survivor of an airplane crash or the one soldier in a battalion who escapes an attack unharmed. It applies in the economic sense to the employee who survives the downsizing of a company like Chrysler, the closing of a competitor on Main Street, or loss of a family member's job. Survivor guilt plays out in our stores when we project our concerns onto our customers; it's like the salesperson adopts a loser's limp. On an irrational level, these individuals wince at their privileged escape from death's clutches—or worry they are next.

Three Types of Survivor Guilt that Affect Sales

1. **I caused it.** Thinker employees believe that they contributed to the failure of their business and are, therefore, risk averse where they once were fearless.

2. **If only.** If only they had done something differently, they personally wouldn't be in the mess they are in. Or, if only they had been able to predict the future, their partners, siblings, or friends would still have jobs.

3. **I need to save them from themselves.** Feelers fear that the customer doesn't need or can't afford these products; so the employee steers them to the cheapest products.

But there's one more type that's especially insidious: self-image.

In the film *Ruthless People,* a stereo salesman played by Judge Reinhold is trying to take advantage of a customer but reneges when he sees that the guy's wife is pregnant. This character feels that the sales process is a win-lose situation—that he is receiving a lot of money for customers' receipt of little value. Let's be candid: this is a common trait in retail, and it occurs more often than we acknowledge.

I was recently on a conference call with the executive team from a huge casino on the Las Vegas Strip about a business makeover. The VP of Sales asked me if I knew what challenges the resort had. I replied, "Revenues are down, so you're probably offering promotions to get people into the restaurants and bars on your property—loss leaders in the hopes of increasing sales. But your servers are only selling the discounted products, and you're not making up the profits." She said, "You're dead right. How did you know that?" I replied, "Because your servers are thinking 'I wouldn't pay 12 bucks for that drink or 30 bucks for that dinner. I couldn't afford it; I'm sure they can't either.' It's a classic case of survivor guilt."

Survivor guilt is a symptom; at the heart of the problem is the fact that Amiable employees feel like shams selling in retail. They're most comfortable with clerking, because their self-image doesn't allow them to put themselves out there to risk rejection.

But showing employees that selling can be a win-win situation is a training opportunity for you and your company. After all, we are helping the customer buy what they already want. You're not manipulating people, taking advantage, or making them into some kind of suckers for purchasing the premium items. We are all grown-ups, and no one knows what another can or cannot afford. Maybe a customer switched to generics for all of her grocery staples to afford the $100 LEGO Death Star for her daughter's birthday. There's no way of knowing this.

To overcome survivor guilt, you also need to show your salespeople how their own preconceived ideas, biases, and fears could be pouring a bucket of water on a customer's flames of interest in the higher-priced items, thereby causing the customer to question the purchase. I witnessed a customer at a coffeehouse pick up a pound of $50-per-pound coffee and tell her friend how much she was looking forward to giving it as a gift. She then turned to the employee behind the counter and asked, "Is this Jamaican Blue Mountain Coffee really that good?" The bitter employee answered, "Not really; you can get about the same taste with one of our $11 coffees." She put the coffee down and left. That is the opposite of what you expect from a sales team. All the employee had to say to make the customer comfortable with her decision to purchase was, "Yes, we sell a lot of it."

If an employee can't overcome his personal low self-esteem when working in retail, you have to ask yourself: "Do I want to let his issues about self-image affect my profitability?" If you've had it, it may be time to consider whether there's anybody else out there who enjoys retail and can help you sell at a profit. Trust me, there is.

On the occasions when employees are not performing, I ask owners to differentiate, "Is this a will issue or a skill issue?" A skill issue is easily corrected by training. But a will issue is not, and you need to deal with this immediately.

It's often said that the speed of the leader is the speed of the group. As the manager, you need to maintain a positive attitude and know how to sell so that you can model for others. This gives you the authority to run your store like a captain instead of a passenger. You should be able to look around your store or restaurant at any point and know who has been waited on, who was waiting on that individual, and where an employee is in the sales process. Once you understand that, you're able to recognize when something goes wrong.

Getting Rid of Dead Weight

What happens, though, when employees aren't self-motivated, and mystery shops or written reviews show that they aren't working out? Your business' greatest asset is its employees. Unlike customers, lease terms, and drive-by traffic, your employees are the one thing you can *control*—at all times. They are a huge liability if they are tardy, uncooperative, have bad attitudes, or simply can't sell. But no one enjoys confronting another person, especially if they are a Feeler. Therefore, we often try to dodge the situation by adopting a passive-aggressive attitude and trying to get the problem employee to quit.

Case in point: I had moved up the ladder at Howard and Phil's Western Wear and had become the regional supervisor of Mark, the manager at the Santa Monica Place location. I knew he wanted to get rid of a particular part-time saleperson because all she did was sort, stack, and size the clothing racks. She hadn't gotten the message to leave, Mark told me later.

One morning, Mark told this salesperson to take all six round racks of Levi's jeans off their hangers, fold them, and put them on shelves by pocket style and size. She finished the task by noon and proudly came back and told Mark, "I'm all done! Now what?" Mark walked over to the wall where the hundreds of jeans were neatly arranged, took both hands, and threw them all on the floor. He then said with a sneer, "Now put them all back on hangers." He did get his wish then; she quit.

I found out that this had happened because the girl's mother called me screaming, demanding to know what kind of man would treat an employee that way. Indeed, there is no reason for this kind of behavior. Mark should have managed the bored Analytical in a different way; and if he couldn't, he should have told her that she wasn't a fit for the position.

Spot Culture Issues before They Intensify

When we don't deal with problems correctly, we can devolve into playing tit-for-tat—as evidenced in this story of a particular manager's passive-aggressive behavior. The manager told his assistant manager:

"The regional supervisor's coming by tomorrow, so I need you to get the following checklist done before you leave. If you have to stay late, that's okay; everything must look perfect for him. Since he's coming in at 10, we won't have a chance to do any of these things in the morning." The assistant manager nodded her head, but only finished half of the items on the checklist.

The next morning when the manager came in, he found boxes of product still on the floor. He called the assistant manager and asked, "Why didn't you get this done last night?" She replied, "We were really busy." The manager looked at the POS system and found few sales. He quickly moved the boxes out of sight just as the regional supervisor entered.

A couple days later, after the manager posted the schedule for the next two weeks, the assistant manager came to him and said, "You have me working on Saturday, but I told you that I needed that day off."

The manager said, "Yes, but Janis can't work and I need you to fill in."

"But it's the big homecoming dance at school," his salesperson pleaded.

The manager replied, "Yes, I'm sorry; but that's all I can do."

The manager should have given a write-up to the assistant manager with clear expectations from the start instead of punishing her by having her work on a day she had specifically requested to take off.

What does a miserable employee look like? I have a survey on my web site that asks, "Is it time to fire your employee?" (www.retaildoc .com/ firing-quiz). Here's how managers who took the survey responded:

- ◆ 56% said the problem employee was either occasionally late or rarely on time.
- ◆ 53% said they had to "grin and bear" working with the employee.
- ◆ 54% said the employee's attitude was "hit or miss" and generally unpredictable.
- ◆ 45% said the employee's supervisor had to constantly talk to them about some correction.
- ◆ 43% said the employee told customers and coworkers something was always wrong, and bad luck was their life.

- 43% said the employee neglected to return calls from supervisors or customers.
- 33% said the employee's sales were at the bottom.
- 29% said the employee ignored or clammed up when talking to customers or other employees.
- 28% said the employee had a negative attitude about himself, life in general, the store's products, and/or his job.
- 25% of employers felt that they needed the employee more than the employee needed the job.
- 24% said they hated the thought of having to work with this employee.
- 24% said that a supervisor or customer had noticed errors committed by the employee.

Here's the scary thing: only 27% of the survey respondents had given staff members at least one written performance review with a deadline. 10% checked "Should I?" (see Figure 6.4).

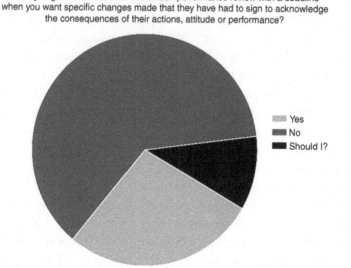

FIGURE **6.4** Firing Poll Results

So even though respondents were unhappy about some of the most basic things about their employees, they either feared rejection or didn't value the employee enough to try to get them to change.

An employee isn't like a spouse or family member with whom you want to work to improve or save a relationship. An employee is simply someone who works at your store. So if an employee isn't performing well and can't seem to get it, you need to give him a sign at some point that you're serious—as well as a chance to correct his performance. The best way to do that is with a written warning.

Written Warnings

There is an art to writing up an employee. You must remove all emotion and generalities from the equation and use a simple, analytical just-the-facts approach. For example: "Joan has arrived 10 minutes late three times in the past week" is much clearer than a weak account that says, "Joan's tardy a lot." You want to be as specific as possible and, as in your training, avoid shades of gray.

The second element is to establish how the employee's behavior has affected your business, and in particular, if there was a monetary component. Continuing with Joan in our example, we might write, "Her tardiness has resulted in having to pay two other staff members overtime to cover her shift." While this will help you challenge a potential unemployment claim, it also helps the employee see how she is damaging your business.

The third element is to let your employee know what the consequences will be if she doesn't change her behavior. If your employee gets three written warnings on the same issue over a short period of time, the fourth should be handing over a final paycheck. You want to increase consequences incrementally. Your first written warning might say, "Joan has to be on time as it states in her signed job description. If this doesn't happen, she may have her hours cut." A second warning might say, "This is the second written warning Joan has had. Further instances of tardiness will lead to loss of hours, shifts, or dismissal." A third would simply state: "The next time Joan is late, she will be dismissed." You rarely get to the third warning; most employees get the idea by this point.

You'll often find when you let someone go that he has been searching for a new job for weeks prior. The body should follow immediately when the mind goes—not six weeks later. The fact that your job is of secondary importance to your employee becomes apparent through issues like attendance and accuracy of orders. A written warning can show the individual what he needs to work on, that you value him, or—if necessary—prepare him for the door. You can find an example of the kind of warning I use online; details are at the end of the book.

Firing Bitter Betty

Many owners and managers are so reluctant to fire employees that they put up with *anyone*. When I tell them to get rid of Bitter Betty, as I call her—the one who the Amiable owner knows she has to fire, the one she hates working with, the one who attracts problems—I often get the retort, "You don't understand, Bob. I can count on her. She's there every day at 10 A.M." And my response is, "Exactly; she's there every day turning customers off." You *know* you have one of these employees right now who needs to go. I even had a franchisee call me crying one time asking me to fire her Bitter Betty for her because the franchisee was, as she claimed, "scared of her." Yikes. Here's how to cut an employee like this loose.

After you've given this person your written warnings, call your accountant or paycheck company and order his final check. Call the employee and tell him there's a schedule change and you're taking him off for the next three days. This both allows for the final check to arrive and essentially forces you to go through with it; after all, he can't keep working if you've taken him off the books. When he shows up to work the next scheduled day, hand him his check and tell him his services are no longer needed.

Don't get into why and how badly you feel, or how it's not his fault, or blame it on the economy. Stand whenever possible to help keep it short and sweet. If the individual has personal items to collect, supervise his packing and escort him to the door.

One of the benefits of letting someone go is that it tunes up your entire team. You don't want to get into specifics about why you fired the colleague, but you can always remind people how important being on time is.

Terri Johnson, owner of Sew Special Studio, sent me the following e-mail recently: "You probably don't remember, but a few years ago when you spoke at the Brother Convention, I spoke with you at the break about a Bitter Betty store manager. You told me in 30 seconds, 'Get rid of her.' I tried to argue, but you just repeated yourself. Well, as scary as it was—I finally did it! It was the best move I've made in the business, with just a little fallout. And only *after* she was gone did I realize that she was driving off business and stealing from me. The stories began to come out of the woodwork!"

Don't let the fear of your former employees receiving unemployment or taking your entire crew with them dissuade you from doing the right thing. There's always someone better waiting to work for you. For that very reason, never stop hiring.

Don't Piss 'em Off

One Saturday night, the Thinker partner of a restaurant went in to grab a cup of coffee. Upon arriving, he heard loud music that was not part of their approved Muzak system. He went in the back, took out the CDs, and asked the employee who was currently working—Mark—whose they were. Upon hearing that the CDs belonged to Mark himself, the Thinker partner took them, threw them in the safe, and told Mark to ask his manager for them back on Monday.

The next week, the manager of the restaurant was counting the cash dropped in the safe and noticed it smelled weird. She thought there must have been an animal in the safe; it actually smelled like urine. She asked the assistant manager if she knew anything about it. The assistant told her that all she knew was that Mark had acted funny when he quit the day before. "Right

before leaving, he took a cup with him to the bathroom. He came
back and I didn't notice what happened, but he went in the back,
clocked out, and left."

Well, what had happened was that Mark relieved himself in
the cup—and poured it into the safe. The Thinker owner had
pissed him off, and Mark had done something to get back at
him. These are the kind of things that happen when a person
who lacks good people skills doesn't change the way he
talks to the various personalities and gets involved in managing
your team.

Make It Work

Successfully managing your crew is not easy; as we've seen, employees with different personality types work in different ways. There are
always a couple of very good salespeople whose numbers are regularly at the top and who are trying to outdo each other. Then there is
the one Analytical salesperson who quietly does his own thing and
gets big sales. There is the Expressive new kid who knows nothing,
but has all the enthusiasm in the world and moves tons of merchandise. There is the Driver who will do anything to be number one. And
then there is the clueless trainee who you wish you'd never hired in the
first place.

You have to broaden your coaching tactics to bring employees to
your breast, not punch them with your fist. It takes planning, training,
and reviewing—and if you have someone who isn't working out, don't
let the person linger, just get rid of him. You'll feel better and he won't
frustrate the rest of the crew or your customers.

You'll find some of my observations about the best salespeople
and how they got that way in the Appendix. Feel free to copy and post
by your employee notices.

Can your employees really "wow" customers while increasing
your store's revenue? They can—if they learn how to go beyond being
clerks to being *salespeople.*

STAT: Five Things to Do Immediately after Reading This Chapter

1. Write out an employee meeting agenda and schedule it.
2. Review the past three months' sales for everyone on your sales floor—that includes you.
3. Give all of your employees a written review.
4. Identify who is not pulling his or her weight and give them a written warning.
5. Put a hiring sign in your window.

Chapter 7

What You Don't Know about the Web Could Kill You

When we're taking care of our health, we start by making sure that the most basic and necessary systems are working. If, for example, you have weak vital signs, poor blood flow, fragile body structure, and impaired lungs—then whether you need glasses is completely immaterial.

In the same way, no amount of promotions, events, or buzz can change a store's unwelcoming exterior, shoddy facility, or bored employees; that's why marketing is the last place to look to improve your financials. Now that we've performed triage on the customer experience and your four walls, an examination of your marketing tactics will show how well you recognize opportunities, bring in new customers, and help current customers spread the word about your great operation.

With so many tools to draw people to you rather than you trying to find them, this chapter will help you see the Internet in a new light. You'll learn about what I call Tier One Marketing—a combination of elements such as the right key words, your web site, a blog, and Google Local to deliver customers who have an immediate desire for your product. Then we'll explore Tier Two Marketing, which speaks to customers not necessarily searching you out today, but who might have intent to shop with you in the future. You'll learn how Facebook fan pages, YouTube, and Twitter can all help you gain buzz, grow fans, and grow sales. Don't worry, it won't get too technical, and a bonus is that all of them are *free*.

We'll touch on pay-per-click advertising and why you should probably not use it. You'll learn why it is smarter to use something similar on Facebook, where more than 400 million Feelers are just waiting to be marketed to. You'll have an easy-to-use table comparing all the ways you can lead customers to your site and the key benefits of each. Finally, we'll talk about some of the more traditional or old-school marketing tactics and how to modify them to your advantage.

The difference between being in print and online is the difference between opening a door and yelling into a dark room, "Where are you?" and opening a door to a well-attended party and announcing, "I'm here!"

Picture a busy freeway full of cars; these are your customers on the Internet. People are buzzing by quickly, trying to get to a specific exit. Now picture yourself standing on the side of the road waving your direct-mail piece trying to get their attention. Where are your customers' eyes on the Internet freeway? Straight ahead toward their destination. Even if you jump up and down and paint yourself red trying to stop them, they are not going to pay attention until they reach their exit. That's the point at which you can capture their interest, because they have arrived.

The Internet freeway is the browser page into which your potential customers type their search terms. Once the search engines have delivered their search results on another page, that's the exit ramp; could be your blog, your web site, or Google Local. That is when customers are interested in who is on those search results; *only* once they've arrived. Make sense?

Tier One Marketing is to get in front of people looking for your products or services by being in the top three search results. Think of it as providing loaves of bread to people searching for bread; it's immediate, tangible, and fills their immediate desire for a specific product or service.

Tier One Marketing—Your Web Site

I'm always surprised to discover that about 30 percent of attendees at my keynote speeches don't have a web site. If you are one of this

30 percent, let me be clear, the Internet is not a storm. A storm is something that you're waiting for to pass, and you know when it's over that you'll be okay. The Internet is a radical change; as big as the Ice Age in terms of the information world. It has completely transformed the way we play the game of marketing—forever.

So—*do* you have a web site? Thinkers, if you do, you'll probably want to skip ahead a few paragraphs to where I talk about key words. Feelers, if you don't have one now, you might fear the process. Relax, there are resources you can visit like www.godaddy.com. Registering your web site address is not expensive, only about $10.

Your web address is the Uniform Resource Locator, commonly known as the URL (for example, www.yyy.com). Your URL should be as original as your name and probably the same as your business's name. Remember, you are going to have this web site for a long time, and you're going to need to give people a site address that is memorable and not complicated. Therefore, avoid hyphens, dashes, and easily misspelled words or confusing spellings (like two repeated s's.) Better yet, create a URL that gives searchers what they are looking for as the address. For example, www.kitchenmixerreviews.com could be much stronger than www.janescookware.com because search engines scan URLs first. It would see those words and deliver it higher on the results page for people searching for kitchen mixer reviews. While Janes Cookware may indeed be the business's name, it would only appear on top of the search results if someone already knew the exact name of the business—and searchers often don't.

If you enter your URL at Go Daddy, it will search and tell you if it is available or not. If yours is taken—like our mixer URL example—consider adding "site" after the name so it will achieve the same ranking. Our example becomes www.kitchenmixerreviewsite.com

While Go Daddy can create an Internet site for you, I suggest a longer-term solution of hiring an outside company to help you develop a web strategy. This endeavor requires a lot of effort, and using someone like a friend or a relative's child oftentimes leads to delays and errors. A good site could cost you anywhere from $500 to $5,000, depending upon the number of pages and the amount of features you want to have. You must have one; don't be penny-wise and pound-foolish. A great web site levels the playing field; you can get visitors just like your bigger competitors. A good online resource for finding people to help you build a site is www.elance.com.

While you can have someone do the work for you, you need to understand that your site is your front door and realize what is important and what isn't—so read on.

KEY WORDS

Google prides itself on being 98 percent correct when you put your search terms into its browser. To stay with our freeway analogy, when you tell your GPS, "I want exit 151" your device delivers the message "I know exactly where 151 is, and using satellites, will take you there." Google navigates by search terms, also called "key words."

A key word (why they don't call it a search word, I don't know) creates the exit ramps. If I type in "outdoor furniture Toledo, Ohio," those four words are the destination I want Google to bring back to me. The more specific the key words, the more targeted the search. This example yielded 24,200 results—still a lot for both you and the search engine to sift through. How can it possibly show all of those? It can't. Therefore, it has to rate sites on criteria and then position them accordingly.

Five Things that Determine Your Web Site Ranking

- ◆ First is your URL.
- ◆ Second are your key words.
- ◆ Third is the title bar of your home page.
- ◆ Fourth is your source code, also called the meta description tags.
- ◆ Fifth, the text on your home page; particularly the first paragraph.

Now take a blank piece of paper and come up with all the possible search terms or key words you think customers would use to find your business on the Internet. Then sit down for a half hour in front of your computer and actually search those terms to see what comes up. Part of this process is to see where you rank on the search but also who the search engines think are your competitors. Once you have a list that you feel represents your customers, go to https:// adwords.google.com/select/KeywordToolExternal and enter each of the key words from your list. This site will tell you how many people actually searched for those key words as well as come up with some variations for you to consider. For example, "People who look for construction tools often look for this. . . ." It's a great resource to verify that enough people are searching for the key words you've identified on your list. You'll either find you were right on the money, or perhaps, if you are a toy store, for example, that no one is looking for "toys without batteries." You can then try to find more meaningful key words that draw them in like "learning toys." Next, prioritize your list with the number one most searched key word at the top; you'll want this to be first whenever you use key words. While you can find niche markets by using key words that are not necessarily the most popular, you want to fish where the fish are first, not swim in your own pool.

TITLE BARS

To receive higher rankings on the search results, the title bar of your site—the blue underlined text (also called a hyperlink) that is displayed in the search engine results page—must be key word-rich. Users click on this hyperlink to visit your web site, so the title bar needs to help Google, Yahoo!, Bing, and the other search engines find your site quickly through the rush hour of the Internet. Let me show you how.

Do you remember the plane that went down in the Hudson River in January of 2009? Go to your computer and enter this URL: http:// blogs.wsj.com/middleseat/2009/01/16/pilot-chesley-'sully'-sullenber ger-what-role-did-glider-flying-play/. (This is very important—don't read on until you are at that page.) Notice the title that's at the very top of the page in gray. "Pilot Chesley "Sully" Sullenberger; What Role Did Glider Flying Play?" Those key words tell Google that this is what you are going to find on that page.

FIGURE 7.1   The *Wall Street Journal* Story Page

When someone is searching, "Sullenberger," "Pilot Chesley," or "role glider played," any of those search words are going to deliver that page (see Figure 7.1).

A key word-rich title bar is vital, yet 80 percent of small business web sites don't use specific key words in their title bars, which makes their chances of being found by the search engines remote, which in turn means they are nonexistent to their web-surfing customers.

Your home page is your welcome mat, your address, your sign in front of your business, which makes it the most important page to build. One of the biggest sins to find in the title bar is displayed in Figure 7.2.

Notice the bar at the top where it says, "Home"? Don't do that. Titling your home page "Home" will cause Google and the rest of the search engines to ignore your site and only include your site in searches for "home"—something that will bury you under hundreds of thousands of real estate sites.

We see this most commonly when a business owner has his son or daughter, boyfriend, or boyfriend's daughter's friend create his site, because they never go back and create a different title bar for each page based on the contents. As Julia Roberts famously said in the movie *Pretty Woman* to the saleswoman who ignored her: "*Big mistake.*"

Your title bar should read like a concise sales pitch of your business to a new customer. The words should flow naturally, as though you were speaking to someone in person, and should be no more than 90 characters. For example, consider the title bar for a party

FIGURE 7.2   A Rotten Title Bar

store that reads, "Big Top Tent Rentals Welcome." How many people are searching for "welcome?" Not a one. This title bar fails, because it doesn't mention where Big Top Tent Rentals *is* or what other services it provides. But they probably referred to it as the "welcome page" when they were creating their site.

To become a student of title bars, go to the big guys like CNN, the *Wall Street Journal,* or Amazon and notice the key words that are in the home page title bars. Click on an article and see how the title bars change to reflect what is on that specific page. Remember that search engines like Google are looking for a 98 percent match, so if the title bar matches the search terms, the search engine will then dig further to see how close a match the key words are used throughout the page. In short, it wants consistency. Think of your home page as one big bucket. Each page you add is a smaller bucket that gets filled from the home page. Make sense? Once you get the hang of all this, you'll be an expert in no time.

Let's stay with the party supply example for a key word-rich home page. Once your home page, the main bucket, is 100 percent, create the smaller buckets or specific pages on your site that feature one type of profitable products. Maybe you want a page that focuses only on party decorations and another on latex balloons in 500 colors. You want to target key words that are specific to that particular page's topic and place these in the title bar for that page. Got it? That's why you want to brainstorm all the pages your site could have before you start building it. You want to hit the bull's-eye for customers looking for what you offer, not fire into the air randomly like many print ads used to do.

A quick recap: Search engines run by key words; they scan the URL and then the title bar of each page. You can take out as many pay-per-click ads as you want, but if you miss either of those first steps, your business will appear further down the search page results— an expensive mistake. I know because I did it myself in the beginning.

When the Internet first started catching on in the 1990s, you could repeat key words over and over in the title bar. Now search engines see that and say, "Those repeated words appear to be spam. I don't like it so that site will appear further down the results page."

Now we have to figure out how we are going to tell Google and the other search engines even more about your site, and that is through something called the source codes. Breathe, Feelers; this is how you'll get more customers to come visit and buy from your store.

SOURCE CODES

The source codes are the key words hidden behind the site that are built on something called meta description tags. Search terms, key-words, meta description tags—all the same. Got it? So why do you need meta description tags if they are identical? Glad you asked.

There are programs called spiders and robots that run across the Internet looking for URLs, title bar key words, and meta description tags in the code of sites. They report their results back to the search engines; that is called "indexing" a site. You can easily find the source code for any page. Let's return to the *WSJ* story example about the Hudson River landing at http://blogs.wsj.com/middleseat/2009/01/16/pilot-chesley-'sully'-sullenberger-what-role-did-glider-flying-play/.

From the top of your browser window, click view, then read down until you see view source. This is the source code for that page; it's the information for the search engines that describes what they are going to find at this address: <meta name="description" content="One of the more interesting elements on the resume of Capt. Chesley 'Sully' Sullenberger—the pilot at the helm of US Airways flight 1549—is his training flying gliders." Notice how the words flowed naturally? Those are the search terms/key words for which the *WSJ* thinks most people will be searching, and they are what Google will use to bring people to this one page at the *Wall Street Journal.*

Take a look at my site, www.retaildoc.com, which I open with, "I'm glad you found my web site for retail sales training and market-ing." The number one search term for the retail doc web site is "retail sales training," the very same key words you'll find in my title bar and meta description tags.

You don't have to know much more about meta description tags—except that if you don't build it with these important key words, your site will not rank as high and you will get fewer visitors.

A final reason that many existing web sites do not get higher search ranking results is because they try to be everything to everybody. They put a laundry list of unrelated key words into their title bar, meta description tags and first paragraph like, "we sell party supplies, balloons, paper plates, streamers, gifts, flowers"—everything but the kitchen sink. Search engines don't like this; remember, they want to be 98 percent accurate when they deliver specific search results.

Spying on Competitors Is Good

A nice thing about checking the view source for meta description tags is that you can spy on your competitors' web sites and copy most of their key words. A good one will have done much of the work for you.

Home Page Text

Many business owners write home page text that reads something like, "Since 1945, we've been a family business concerned with making every customer feel valued and welcome to our store." What a waste of real estate! That text actually *hurts* you, because it doesn't contain any key words that describe your business for search engines to match. The search engines' robots and spiders will conclude that it's not a good match and lower your position in search engine rankings.

Your first paragraph must be a summary of what you do using relevant key words. Search engines don't give a darn that you're Chaney and Vinny and that you started your company with your mom in your garage. They don't care that you "value your customers every day and offer gift wrapping"—and neither do your potential customers, because they aren't searching for any of those words.

Revisit the list of key words you created earlier and write out what you do in two concise, key word-rich sentences. Information like being a family business or the number of years you've been around is not important to someone who will only scan your page for three seconds at most before clicking away; you can put that information farther down the page. You want your site visitors to stick around, and that will only happen if they quickly see something in those first few lines that matches what they are searching for.

As you get more advanced, you'll want to use hyperlinks on each page to refer to other pages on your site; take a look again at the www .retaildoc.com site as an example.

Finally, all of the text on your home page should be built on the same key words. After your domain name, title bar, and meta description tags, the first paragraph is the next place that Google checks to make sure the site is a match for the key words. All of that drives traffic to the main bucket: your domain's home page. Before you think about Facebook, Twitter, or other online sites, fix your web site with the right key words. Once all of that is done, you must list your site with Google Local.

GOOGLE LOCAL BUSINESS CENTER—THE YELLOW PAGES ON STEROIDS

Google Local Business Center (LBC) is a feature that uses GPS-like tracking of a searcher's logon location to deliver local results. Registration is necessary but free; go to http://tinyurl.com/3a8sh4 and follow the instructions. Don't do this before your site is properly created and ready to go, otherwise you might not end up as high in Google's local rankings.

Google will ask that you verify yourself as the business owner, either by phone or by postcard. Choose the phone option so there is no delay—just be sure you are the one who answers the phone in the next several hours! Once verified, you can include payment options, hours of operation, up to 10 photos, and as many as five YouTube video links. You don't have to do it all at once, and you can always edit any errors. Once you've done that, check Google Maps to search using your key words, city, and state to see where you end up (see Figure 7.4).

Google Maps   **Local Business Center**

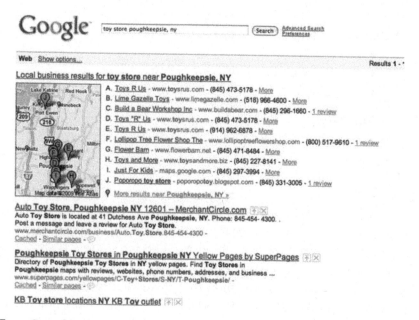

After about a month, you must make sure to check the Google LBC statistics and results of the key word searches to fine-tune your home page text. You can even find out the zip codes associated with requests for driving directions to your business—which is incredibly important if you want to advertise or when you cross-promote with other businesses.

Wrap-Up: Using Google Local Business Center

The Pros

◆ Lets anyone searching for your key words easily find you.

◆ Allows links to video.

◆ Allows pictures.

◆ Shows up on Google and other search engine results.

(continued)

(*continued*)
  ◆ Is trackable.
  ◆ Can be done in a half hour or less.
  ◆ Is totally free.

The Cons
  ◆ None.

Blogs

Once your site is fully search engine optimized with key words, fresh content is a good way to increase your results page ranking, and one way to do this is with a blog. Short for web log, a blog is an online journal where you can post entries about your business. A good example of a major brand's blog that mixes text well with images and video is http://1000words.kodak.com/. While that's not where you need to be yet, it shows what is possible.

A blog is easy to set up using sites like Wordpress.com, TypePad .com, or others that are recommended to you. Rather than take up a lot of time discussing how to start blogging, I'm going to recommend you visit the paid site http://tinyurl.com/starturblog. It covers the basics really well, and if you prepay for six months, they will build the blog for you with all the bells and whistles.

But what are you going to write about? Go back to your key words. Each posting should contain at least a couple of those. In blogging, we call key words "tags." Got it? Search words equal key words equal tags. When you create a post, you want to take the time and effort to connect with individuals and not be vanilla. So take a stand, make a confession, or share an insight.

For example: Kirsten Mead—owner of a craft store called About Memories and More—contacted me about the struggles she was encountering with her store. I suggested that she write about this topic on her blog instead of chronicling another craft project. While she was initially a bit nervous about being that vulnerable, she took my advice and here is what she wrote back: "You had suggested I write a blog post about things being rough at the store. Here's the link to what

I wrote. It's been out a couple of days, and I'm getting a fantastic response to it. http://tinyurl.com/nklbww. My blog traffic has tripled . . . the kits are selling out . . . and they are excited about creating again. The idea for the 30/30 challenge came about when I was listening to your recommended audio of *The Strangest Secret* . . . something Earl Nightingale said that I'd missed the 100 times before when listening was provide more service and get more return . . . provide less service and get less return. It's true."

Kirsten's struggle resonated with her customers; they saw her as a person, not just someone looking to get their money. Confessions like this will draw Feelers to you and works much better than attempting to push product on them. That's the goal of marketing on the Internet; you want people to be moved, care about you and your business, and recommend it to their friends. Kristen didn't whine and complain but acknowledged how she, too, was struggling; then shared with her readers what she did to overcome it. People want to hear about winning not losing; remember that whenever you refer to your business in an interview, profile, or on your sales floor.

To come up with blog ideas or titles, look to magazine covers at your supermarket checkout counter: *Six Ways to Beat X, How I Stopped Y and Z, Getting Ready for the Holidays.* Your blog should be informal and have a definite point of view. If you haven't checked mine out yet, visit http://www.retaildoc.com/blog for an example.

Remember to pick the same tags as your key words so that the search engines index them, just like your regular web site. Ask your web developer how to host your blog on your web site; this will help your rankings with search engines like Google, Bing, Yahoo!, and others.

COMMENT ON OTHER SITES OR BLOGS TO DRAW PEOPLE TO YOURS

One way to increase your online presence is by increasing the number of unique visitors to your site. This is not the same as "hits"; those include search engines' automated programs that index the sites, not actual people searching for you. Commenting on blogs and articles you read online draws people to your web site. When I find an article in my field of retail sales, I make a two-line comment and put my blog address in the comment box. This has resulted in a huge increase in blog hits. My blog statistics show that searchers visit www.retaildoc .com to learn more about me and my company, sign up for my newsletter, read my materials, hire me to speak at their events, buy my retail sales training videos, teleseminars, or other products.

Even if you don't have a blog right now—if there is relevant information you could add to a story, speak up and post a comment! Just make sure to include the link to the exact page on your site where readers can find the related information (not just your home page). For example, a designer could post a comment on a story about using color in the home like, "Lime green is one of the hot colors for spring, and when paired with navy and white it says, 'fresh, new, spring.' For more free design tips, visit (insert your URL.)" Entering a comment this way allows readers to simply click on the link. Going back to the analogy we used about the freeway exit ramps, the designer would be right where people who are searching for what they offer: design tips.

Once your Tier One Marketing—your web site and Google Local Business Center account—are 100 percent complete, you'll be able to attract people who want to purchase your product or service. Thinkers are more likely to have embraced these necessary steps, whereas Feelers may be overwhelmed by the technical nature of what we've covered so far. Stay with it Feelers; this is the gold you've been missing in your marketing efforts, not another discount coupon offering.

If you are comfortable starting a blog, then by all means, do so; if not, move on to Tier Two Marketing: social media. Whereas Tier One Marketing would be used to attract people specifically searching for loaves of bread to buy, Tier Two is more like scattering your breadcrumbs to get more people to discover you. These people aren't actively or specifically looking to buy your product, but you influence them via social media sites like Facebook, YouTube, and Twitter (see Figure 7.5 on the following page). These sites appeal to searchers' *intent* to buy, and using them gives you a leg up on your competition. Social media will be more exciting for Feelers, because they're connecting with customers in a personal manner. It can seem frivolous for Thinkers, so keep reading Drivers and Analyticals!

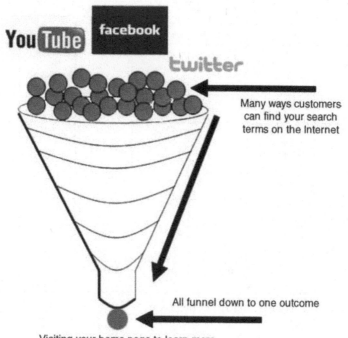

FIGURE **7.5** How Social Media Can Draw Customers to You

I'm going to describe each of these sites in detail to show you how easy they are to use and point out some of their drawbacks and advantages. Because the Web changes at lightening speed, I'll be posting updates to this information after publication of this book to keep you current at www.retaildoc.com/guide/update.php.

Tier Two Marketing—Social Media: Breadcrumbs that Attract Potential Customers to Your Web Site

According to a March 2009 report from research firm Nielsen, two-thirds of the planet's Internet population visits social networking sites. Chances are good that at least some of those are your customers as well.

The Internet has the unique ability to allow you to scatter your breadcrumbs across a wide area to help people find their way to you,

WHERE TO SCATTER YOUR BREAD CRUMBS ACROSS THE INTERNET					
	Your Web Site	Your Blog	Facebook Fan Pages	YouTube	Twitter	Google Local
Upload Photos?	Possible but probably more work than you want to do	Easily	Easily	No	Possible but not in general use	Possible
Post Links?	Yes	Yes	Yes	Yes	Yes	Yes
Post Updates?	No	No	Yes	No	Yes	No
Upload Video	Possible but probably more work than you want to do	No	Yes	Yes	No	Yes
Open to Anyone?	Yes	Yes	No	Yes	Yes	Yes
Search Word Optimized?	Yes	Yes	No	Yes	Yes	Yes
Comments Allowed?	No	Yes	Yes	Yes	Yes	No
Statistics Available?	Yes, unique visitors	Yes, number of views	Yes, number of fans	Yes, number of views	Yes, number of followers	Yes, number of impressions

FIGURE 7.6   How Social Media Sites Compare

so the more you scatter, the better (see Figure 7.6). Unlike those that Hansel and Gretel left, your breadcrumbs will not be devoured by forest creatures so once they've been established, your breadcrumbs should always lead back to your web site. This is an admittedly subjective explanation of three of the biggest sites with which small businesses should be familiar.

FACEBOOK

This is like throwing a party and inviting people to attend.

Facebook fan pages are designed for people who are already interested in you and your company. They share a component of another site, Twitter, which allows you to tell people what's going on in your store in real time. Much like breadcrumbs, your Facebook fan page encourages people to *pull* your information based on what you

post, rather than you *pushing* it out to them like a newsletter or a postcard; the same is true of Twitter and YouTube.

Facebook fan pages let you notify fans about special events, appearances, or reasons you purchased a particular product to offer them. You can also post videos, pictures, start discussions, hold question-and-answer sessions with customers—pretty much anything you'd want to put out there. By interacting in real time, you can listen to actual customers in a way that wasn't possible a mere three years ago. You can also start a group, however, these don't seem to be as valuable as fan pages. You can visit and join mine at www.retaildoc.com/facebook.

Like all social media sites, Facebook helps people who *might* be interested in you. This differs from your web site, where they are specifically searching for your products, services, or business. Be forewarned: Due to its social nature, Facebook can eat away at your day. Give yourself a set time limit—especially Expressives and Amiables.

According to the analytics firm Compete, Facebook had more than 350 million unique visitors as of December 2009, and these aren't just members of the younger crowd. Visitors over age 35 have increased by 23 percent over the same time frame.

While I won't go into detail on how to start a Facebook fan page here, one important thing to know immediately is that you need to set up an individual account first to be able to establish your fan page. This is also incredibly easy. Make sure to fill in your profile completely, with all the details about you and your business plainly laid out for all to see. The profile is just like any other social network profiles you may have on LinkedIn, Twitter, YouTube, Flickr, and so forth.

Once you've established your fan page, invite customers to join. While it's tempting to invite family, what you really want are local customers. When they join, it shows up on their wall, and it also shows up on all their friends' walls, as well. That's how you build the awareness and intent to shop at your store.

Update your fans about what is coming, ask them a question, or start a very easy poll. You could also repost information about your product or vendors—you want to avoid it being all about you and let it be a dialogue. The goal is to listen to your customers so you can do an even better job for them. This requires that you check your Facebook fan page daily and ideally post one thing daily as well, so there is fresh content for fans to view. Stay on topic and avoid the quizzes and other personal stuff—this is business.

One of the things you can do with a Facebook fan page is create paid advertising for the people most likely to respond: your neighbors. You can find this at the very bottom of the page under "Advertising," where you can click to create an ad. (A great resource that explains all of this very well is *The Facebook Era* by Clara Shih, 2009.) Of course, you'll have to come up with something to advertise—maybe an event, a product, or a service and a link back to the exact page on your web site where that item, event, or service can be found. Then you can select Facebook users in your area and include others within 10, 25, or 50 miles of your town. You can select by sex, age, level of education, relationship status, and key words. For example, if you have a product just for dentists, you could enter "dentist" as a key word for your ad. Facebook will scan everyone's profile and updates for the word "dentist" along with your other selections, and only show your ad to those people. If that was your target—even if it was a small number—you're essentially using a laser to hone in on only those local customers most likely to respond to you. That's something the search engine pay-per-click ads can't do at the moment.

Each time you make a selection, Facebook automatically shows you how many people could potentially see your ad. This is a huge improvement over pay-per-click on the major search engines, as you can drop thousands of dollars trying to hit a target that's too large and not really interested in what you have to offer. For that reason, I don't recommend search engine pay-per-click advertising for your retail store.

Once your ad has begun running on Facebook, you can check statistics just like at the Google Local Business Center to determine the ages of people who clicked on your ad, their gender, relationship status—the works. This makes tracking the effectiveness of the method you use to reach your audience much easier. Have an ad that didn't work so well? Go back and tweak it, then check the statistics in a couple days.

Okay, Thinkers: You may be doing what I saw in an *ABC News* piece entitled "The Last of the Facebook Holdouts," and skipping this important marketing platform. The segment highlighted people who were gloating about the fact that they weren't on Facebook. It said in part that these "Web 2.0 teetotalers just don't understand what the fuss is all about. 'Some of the great joys in life are meeting new people in person and people watching, and spending time with my kids, and writing,' said David Vicker, a 37-year-old freelance media producer.'"

Such comments miss the point entirely. Social media isn't an *either*, it is an *and*. You can meet new people in person, spend time with them, *and* be part of various social networks. The Facebook population is now 42 times larger than the population of New York City; its 300 million users would be the fifth largest nation in the world if it were its own country. There are more than 65 million active users currently accessing Facebook through their mobile devices. That's a lot of potential profit improvers for you Thinkers to ignore.

After you use it for at least six months, you might find that Facebook isn't right for you; or worth the effort to come up with postings that engage your fans; you might want to outsource updating it. Your payoff will be nothing like getting your web site perfect— that's why this is Tier Two marketing. However, you should at least *try it* before deciding your customers aren't on there, you don't need it, or whatever lame excuse your lazy butt is comfortable repeating.

Wrap-Up: Facebook Fan Page

The Pros

- ◆ Lets you keep in touch with your very best customers and fans.
- ◆ Provides immediate updates for new merchandise, sales, and events.

(continued)

(*continued*)
- ◆ Offers targeted advertising to within 10 miles of your town by various groups.
- ◆ Has trackability.
- ◆ Can include videos.
- ◆ Customers can post videos and photos as well as give their testimonials.
- ◆ Is totally free.

The Cons
- ◆ People who don't know you probably won't see you unless you advertise.
- ◆ People have to accept your invitation to join them on your personal page.
- ◆ You won't show up on any search other than Facebook.
- ◆ Can be a time-suck, especially for Feelers.

YouTube: Your Own Personal Video Channel

A *Los Angeles Times* music reviewer told a story of riding in the car with his 7-year-old when he put in a CD of one of Bach's Brandenberg Concertos. After it was done he asked his son what he thought of it and his son responded, "It wasn't bad, but what did it look like?"

Video is altering our perception of information. While Facebook connects you with people you generally already know, YouTube lets you take your store, products, and customers to a whole new level online. According to technology blog Tech Crunch, YouTube streams over 1.2 billion videos per day worldwide. That pretty much means that *everyone* on the Internet is watching an average of one YouTube video per day.

The old way was to *tell* people; now you can *show* them and tell your story better with video than print. A few two-minute videos and a YouTube account will get you positioning for your key words quickly and easily. Some of the things you can do on YouTube include:

◆ Recycling your commercials.
◆ Filming store tours.
◆ Instructing customers how to prepare for your product installation.

You can add hundreds of videos at no cost, *and* you get all the benefits of key word searches since Google owns YouTube.

How to Begin Using your key words, brainstorm what people might be interested in. Demand Media has found that video titles that include "best" and "how to" bring in traffic or high click through rates, while "history of" is video poison. Next, get yourself something like a Flip or other portable video camera for under $150. The Flip has a USB plug built in so after you shoot, you can plug into your Mac or PC and the software will let you download and edit the video quickly and easily. I'm sure you can easily search for more tips about how to create videos on YouTube. A major advantage is that you are posting them for free and can link to your other sites like your blog, web site, Google LBC account, or Facebook fan page at no cost, as well.

Make absolutely sure that you fill in the information about your video, including city and state as well as your key words and links. Finally, make sure you have a title card at the front and back and a "lower third" title card across the bottom with your web site so people can find you. If you upload more than one, you can create your own channel for free. You can see an example of mine at www.youtube.com/bobphibbs.

If, for instance, you are a caterer and want to stand out from the competition, you might post a YouTube video of you setting up a party, or one on how to set up a luau, or the three mistakes to avoid when picking a caterer. A restaurant might post short videos of its chef, bartender, or barista making a special or drink of the week. If you are a farmer, post a short video showing who planted your tomatoes or harvested your corn. If you are a hardware store, you might begin your own series of fix-it videos like "How to Fix a Bathroom Towel Bar," "How to Stop a Leaky Faucet," or "How to Knock off Your Honey Do List in One Morning."

No matter what your business, create six or seven YouTube videos as quickly as possible, and include all your contact information on the bottom of the player. And Feelers, please don't get caught up worrying about whether it's professional enough. I spent three hours creating a video that told one woman's story of how she started her business, why people should choose her brand, and how her company was different. She was happy with it until we posted it on YouTube. A few critical friends felt it wasn't good enough, and she pulled it. Now, eight months later, she *still* has nothing up—while competitors have posted nearly 20 clips. Most YouTube videos are purposely amateur looking to seem more authentic; some are now even shot on cell phones.

I know, you might be saying, "But Bob, I don't live in a big city like New York; why would I want to put this out all over the world?" The answer is that people in your hometown use the Internet just as much as anyone else. It's easy enough to find a college student that can create a YouTube video for you—because most of them have already done lots themselves.

You know that old saying, "I know 50 percent of my advertising works; I just don't know which 50 percent"? Well, you can measure just about *anything* online. Zappos reports a 6 to 30 percent increase in sales when the product is featured in a video. Once you get your video up and running and have provided store profile information, you can check statistics just as you can on Google LBC and Facebook fan pages to find the age, gender, location, likes/dislikes, and more of anyone who clicked on your video.

Begin brainstorming some ways that you can show some of the fun aspects of how your business is different.

Wrap-Up: YouTube

The Pros

◆ Lets anyone searching for your key words find you.

◆ Allows links.

◆ Is totally free.

◆ Shows up on Google and other search results.

◆ Is a good way to use existing video in a new forum.

◆ Can be used to host your videos and posted on other sites like Facebook and Google Local Business Center.

The Cons

◆ Can be intimidating to create without help.

◆ You can be your own worst critic.

TWITTER

As opposed to a Facebook fan page where you create a group, Twitter sends you and your business out into the world, and your group forms around you. Twitter allows users to send and receive 140-character updates called "tweets." When you choose to subscribe to someone's updates, you are "following" them. Twitter is different from Facebook because you can follow people without them following you; the relationship does not have to be mutual. Twitter's power comes from being able to expose your brand and expert information to a network of followers. Much like your e-mail list, the more followers you have, the more potential influence you will have to get people's attention. In the United States, Twitter is expected to top 16 million users in 2010, but is still only about 15 percent of Facebook's size.

Thinkers, if you've heard of Twitter before but have brushed it off as pointless—"I don't care about someone telling me they are brushing their teeth"—just stay with me. Originally Twitter was designed to be read on a cell phone so that your friends would know what you were up to while both you and they were on the move. But it's evolved away from chatting with friends; it's now about promoting yourself and your business, and that's why you should consider being on it.

Twitter is growing exponentially. While no one can be sure where it is headed, one thing is clear: several businesses that have embraced it are meeting with great success.

The *Los Angeles Times* featured a story about a Korean barbeque truck called Kogi, a prime example of a business using Twitter to market a great product in a clever and unique way. The mobile diner travels all over the greater Los Angeles area, but the only way to find out its next location is to follow the truck's Twitter feed online (@kogibbq). The feed, which currently has almost 10,000 followers, leaks out the location only several hours in advance—creating a fanatical, cult-like following. Oh and—no discounts.

How Do You Use Twitter?   The first thing to do is to sign up for a free account at http://twitter.com/account/create. Your next stop should be at the Twitter help guide—http://help.twitter.com/portal—to get all of your basic how-to questions answered. Read it; it will save you some time and frustration. After you're done, download a free handbook at www.twitterhandbook.com.

Once you create an account, you will receive a home and profile page. (Find mine for an example at: http://twitter.com/theretaildoctor.) Here, you can find other Twitter streams to follow, post your own messages, and even watch the entire public stream of comments flow by. Be sure to fill in your profile completely. Don't protect your updates, and do list any other web sites you may have, including your home page and blogs.

Not sure what to post? Just write something about what you are doing: "New to Twitter, hoping to learn its secrets before lunch today." It doesn't matter much; just get started. Don't worry, Feelers; you really can't do anything *wrong*.

If you own a restaurant, for instance, you could tweet customers' comments about your food or service, print their tweets on your menu, or write them on the specials board. You could collect Twitter names with the check, and then thank them the next day for coming in via a tweet, and you could also tweet their comments about your restaurant.

Beware, though, that Twitter works both ways; your customers will use this medium to praise *and* criticize. If someone doesn't have a good time at your restaurant, he or she will tweet about it as well, so you'll have to monitor your own name to stay ahead of it.

The big question you may ask at this point is *why would I need to use this?* Here are a few reasons:

- ◆ Do you want to network with others in your industry—either locally or nationally? While this might do you some good, it might take a while to build your network.
- ◆ Are your customers particularly tech-savvy? If so, they will definitely be on Twitter. Of all the social media, Twitter speaks to the Thinkers versus Facebook, which speaks to the Feelers.
- ◆ Do you want to know what's going on in the world with people who share your interests? Twitter is good for that, since many people publish links, content, and other resources in their tweets.
- ◆ Do you have a blog that needs publicity? Twitter can be a good way to get some; just provide the headline and link.
- ◆ Looking for new ways to connect with your customers? Get them to follow you on Twitter. Make sure you post relevant items like new products and links to your online newsletter. The image in Figure 7.10 shows one of my favorites: Pufferbellies toys from Virginia. They post new products and news about other events that are taking place at their toy store to draw people to them. *That* is the future of advertising. If you sell an item that people want fresh—like baked goods or coffee, for example—tweet when your products come out of the oven or roaster.
- ◆ Conduct a Twitter search of your main key words to discover who you should follow and learn what works.

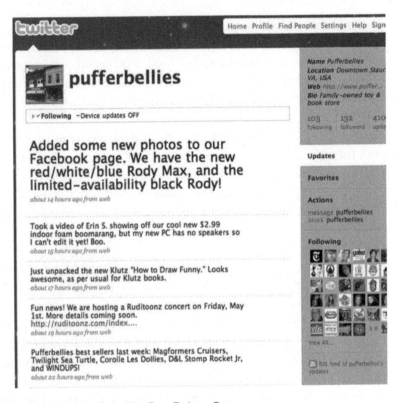

FIGURE **7.10** The Pufferbellies Toys Twitter Page

◆ Do not, however, use Twitter to promote your business to new people. Your posts should not include information like "$50 off this weekend only"; or followers will drop you like a rock. Also, don't use Twitter as an electronic Val-Pak coupon disseminator, as your tweets will become more like spam. Be creative, you have so much more to offer than another Santa Claus promotion giving your profits away. Remember, you're trying to make money in all of this—not give away the store.

Now here's the downside: the average user only has about 10 followers and 60 percent drop out after trying it for a month. For the effort that is required, I would suggest this be *last* on your list of ideas to promote your business—unless you are located in a very tech-heavy area. However, you might also consider setting up an account, if for nothing else than to monitor comments.

Get your social networking sites on everything, including your shopping bags. Include "Follow us on Twitter" with your user name in

---

Wrap-Up: Twitter

The Pros

- Helps anyone searching for your key words or your name find you.
- Allows customized background on your profile page.
- Is totally free.
- Updates can help you connect with new vendors and customers.

The Cons

- Still currently growing; limited number of people on it.
- Potential to have people tell everyone about a bad experience means that you need to monitor.

---

the signature line of your e-mails. Include "Join our Facebook Fan Club" with your unique URL on your web page. Post "Catch our videos on YouTube" in your catalog mailer. Put these messages on your home page, your blog, your receipts, at the bottom of your events calendar—*anywhere* customers could see your message.

Google pay-per-click paid ads used to be the main way to market your company on the Web. Many business owners have tried it, only to end up spending lots of money on low—or no—conversion rates. That's because as great as pay-per-click can be, you have to have a perfect web site for it to really deliver. Because search engines' reach is so vast and key words can be too broad, you often pay a lot in the learning curve. However, if you've done everything else in this chapter and can budget at least $500 a month for it, consider placing pay-per-click ads on Google or the other search engines.

Updating Your Old School Santa Claus Marketing Tactics

Old school marketing meant taking out a display ad in the paper with some type of call-to-action discount. I call it Santa Claus marketing—give it away because you're nice. While many people thought coupon redemptions proved how well their ad worked, it just showed there are cheap people in the world. Internet marketing, on the other hand, is both trackable and cost effective—no discounting required.

Coupons and discounts speak to the Analytical, who thinks: why wouldn't I want to save money? But there is much more to marketing than playing Santa Claus and giving discounts in some misguided attempt to bring paying, profitable customers to your doors. Remember any discounts you offer directly affect your profitability. Coupon users typically go where the hot deal of the moment is and are likely to abandon you for the next deal they're offered. Coupons are used

FIGURE 7.11   You Have to Have More Arrows than Discounts to Reach Profitable Customers

primarily because there is nothing else to bring people back to the business. It's like an archer with only one arrow in his quiver trying to hit the target when he needs a well-stocked variety.

You want customers who are so loyal to your business that they'll drive past a competitor and not think of shopping there—and contrary to all the doom-and-gloom experts, that is still *very* possible. In fact, you probably do it every day with your own favorite store. You need to be everything to someone rather than something to everyone.

If you want to give discounts, only give them to people who have built your business: your loyal customers. They will appreciate the perk and help you stay in business when you're not running sales. And in order to reach them, you need a large list of customers, which, in the old days, would have been your mailing list. However, with so many people standing over the trash as they go through their mail—and as the cost of postage has gone up—a mailing has become quite an expensive proposition. That's why, if you have a physical mailing list, I encourage you to transition to a list of e-mail addresses.

Except in the case of a Grand Opening—when *no one* knows you—you want to only build your list from people who know you and your merchandise and have given you permission to contact them.

How to Convert Your Mailing List to an E-Mail List

Create a postcard and announce an offer on the back: $100 off your next order, or $50 worth of upgrades, or enter to win a trip. It doesn't matter *what* you offer as long as you establish a high value, and it is something your customers will respond to.

Tell them you're going green and transitioning your mailing list to an e-mail list. Make sure you have a place below that for them to enter their e-mail address. Give a date they have to bring it in or mail it back to you, and make sure that it informs them that *winners are notified only by e-mail.* Send the card out to anyone who you've done business with: customers, vendors, neighbors—the works. Do not buy a list. It is a waste of money.

(continued)

> (*continued*)
>
> Here's the secret to making this work. A lot of people who like you and recognize the card will respond, but some won't. That's why you do a duplicate mailing two weeks later (just pull out those who brought in their cards already). It increases response rates by 20 percent.

Otherwise you send out shotgun e-mails that land with a thud or people report you as a spammer.

Just as a mailing list used to be, an e-mail list is a numbers game; the more names you have, the higher you can drive your sales. If every business had the inclination and money, they could determine how much each name delivers in sales. IBM recently concluded that each of its e-contacts was worth $948 for the company—a powerful number. To capture your customers' e-mail addresses, provide a sign-up on the home page of your web site, offer slips people can fill out at your registers, and bring those forms to any event you participate in.

Using an online company like Constant Contact, you can then send out monthly information in a newsletter that keeps you top-of-mind. What to put in your newsletter? To get an idea, look at the magazines in your local supermarket and steal their cover stories. For example, *Five Ways to Make Your Trip to the Beach Perfect* or *Three Overlooked Things to Have at a Party* or *How to Keep Your Coffee Fresh (and it's not in the freezer)*, or *Keeping Your Driveway Clear of Snow*. All of them are informational and will encourage customers, particularly Feelers, to read on. You can have an offer if you wish, but keep it short; too many offers or stories waste customers' time and prompt them to hit delete.

The worst thing to do is to keep inundating customers with another offer for buy-one-get-one-free, 20 percent off this weekend only, free shipping, and the like. It all looks the same after awhile, and there is no value to the customer—so again, they delete. An effective newsletter has to be designed from the viewpoint of a Feeler customer who requires information, not a store owner or manager who requires sales. Hint: use words like "you" and "your" instead of "we" and "I."

Again, marketing to people online is much easier than some of the old-school guerilla marketing methods. Forget sticking fliers on people's cars and hanging offers from their doorknobs. If you want to go door-to-door and introduce yourself, your own shoe leather is a great resource. I walked a half-mile radius from a client who'd been open over 20 years to discover less than a third of his neighbors knew his business. That presented a great opportunity to make a personal connection. If you have the time and can do it when people are home—after work and weekends—this is a good tactic for growing your business. And if you are still taking out Yellow Pages ads, please be aware that no one—other than perhaps your grandmother—is looking for anything besides *maybe* a plumber. Save your money, and cancel that Yellow Pages contract *now*.

What about Newspapers?

Much has been written about the end of the newspaper business but there are still places newspapers can be effective:

- Community newspapers that have a small distribution area around your location.
- Big metropolitan newspapers for a yearly sale or if you have multiple spread-out locations.
- Online editions where you can advertise to neighbors who know you.

News is still big business; they are trying to find different avenues to connect with readers—like retailers looking for customers.

The old way that marketing was conducted was to interrupt customers while they were pursuing other interests; think TV commercials in the middle of your favorite program, magazine ads in the middle of a celebrity profile, newspaper ads making you turn back and forth between pages. You had to put up with them if you wanted to read the article or see the show. Interruption marketing is the past; the future of marketing is *participation*. Using Tier Two Marketing can help you monitor your brand, engage your customers, and give you a direct link to what customers are looking for. To get them to your door to begin with though, you need to have all of the Tier One Marketing running perfectly.

STAT: Five Things to Do Immediately after Reading this Chapter

1. Make a plan to grow your e-mail list to a couple thousand addresses.
2. Get a web site—Tier One Marketing.
3. Brainstorm key words.
4. Register for Google Local Business Center.
5. Try one of the Tier Two Marketing strategies like YouTube or Facebook.

Chapter 8

It's Up to You Now

After you've been to the doctor for a checkup and you receive the news about what is ailing you, your doctor would prescribe the treatment, how to monitor your progress, and send you on your way. If, however, your diagnosis is a serious disease, there would be three ways you could approach the news:

1. Like Rocky Balboa in *Rocky*, with an "I'm going to win" attitude and taking steps to train yourself to overcome any weakness.
2. Deny its seriousness and convince yourself that it's not that bad, like the Black Knight in *Monty Python and the Holy Grail* who claimed that "It's just a flesh wound"—while you continue to bleed profits.
3. Identify with it and become mired in all of its related issues, like an elderly relative who constantly complains that "I'm really sick," as he details every ailment big and small—and become overwhelmed; helpless.

My goal for you, of course, is to choose option number one. Throughout this book, you have been on a search to increase profits, and you've discovered hundreds of choices and opportunities that can get you there. You've seen how easy much of it is—and how attainable. So ask yourself, what radical change do you need to implement to ensure your success? Do you have the guts to throw out what you've been doing and start over?

Former CEO of Arrow shirts Roger Leithead told me how his company embraced change during the Great Depression. The Arrow shirt concept originated in the 1800s when men, even the blacksmiths, only wore white dress shirts. One blacksmith was a singer as well, and his wife didn't like him coming home and changing into a clean shirt just to go to church choir practice. Since they only bathed on Saturday nights, the shirt would be dirty and she would have to wash it again by hand. She came up with the idea of a detachable collar and cuffs, which made it easy to look presentable without all that washing and saved many of the fragile pearl shirt buttons from breaking.

This system of collars and cuffs is the foundation upon which Arrow built an empire of over 450 warehouses across the United States filled with detachable collars and cuffs. It was a recipe for success: find out what customers want and then give it to them.

Then the Manhattan Shirt Company came out with a shirt that featured an *attached* collar and cuffs. It was built like a tent with yards of fabric to tuck in. Men had to wear armbands, like you now see in barbershop quartets, so their sleeves wouldn't reach over their fingers. That was based on need as well, since shirts only had one size 37-inch sleeve length. They needed to make them that way because the shirt shrank with every washing.

By 1930, Arrow profits were dropping off and the CEO saw that the trend was changing to a complete shirt with no removable pieces. He announced to his board of directors, "We will never get there doing what we're doing now." That's when something truly remarkable happened. He went downstairs and instructed his employees to open the doors of their Hudson riverfront warehouse and "clear it out." The warehouse men used pitchforks to throw all of the existing collars and cuffs into the river.

Forget the environmental consequences of more than one million collars and cuffs floating down the Hudson; the company's CEO threw out its *entire inventory* in order to make the changes needed.

Arrow then came up with 64 combinations of neck and sleeve lengths to make sure that, unlike the competitors' sack, its shirts would fit properly. Arrow changed from natural ocean pearl buttons that broke easily to plastic and invented Sanforizing, which meant its shirts wouldn't shrink. Arrow again became the leader in men's shirts, because its CEO realized that the company had to change or die.

You think it's tough to compete now? Imagine going into a retailer during the Depression, when one in four men were unable to find a job, and telling the buyer that while three models could previously capture the market, they now needed *64*.

The CEO had the marketing department come up with the "Arrow Shirt Man." Splashy ads in the best women's magazines touted how well an Arrow shirt fit. Wives responded by going into retailers and asking for "that Arrow shirt." Retailers had no choice but to carry the entire inventory; the company flourished because Arrow embraced change.

Many businesses didn't make much of a profit in the past few years when the money was easy. Now that money is tighter, many more are struggling. They didn't see the recession or additional competition as anything requiring them to change. Many dropped their prices and figured that would draw customers to them. When it didn't, some talked about how unfair business was to the independent, or stressed "buy local" programs thinking this mattered to most customers. It doesn't. You shouldn't try to guilt customers into buying because that is really about a *business's* need for cash, not the *customers'* need for an exceptional shopping experience. Buy local programs alone can't do the heavy lifting of bringing customers back to your store time and time again.

Many stores wasted precious time they could have used to make themselves stronger. They exhibited the *hubris* spoken about in Greek tragedies—a feeling that you can make yourself invincible through your own actions. Hubris boasts, "Oh, I have loyal customers." But loyal customers are few and far between nowadays without a lot of work to keep them. Claiming that your company has great "word of mouth" is not a marketing strategy; it's often a way of kidding yourself.

The only way to thrive as the retail industry goes through a shake-out is to radically alter your business's standards for growing profits, because the customer and her purchases cannot be taken for granted. Using a "buy local" campaign or participating in the excellent 3/50 program are icing on the cake if you are first focused on the customer.

With everyone pinching pennies, a leisurely day at the mall just isn't going to happen any time soon for most people. Likewise, sticking your head in the sand hoping something will change out there, while cutting prices and offering more discounts, is a recipe for disaster.

Case in point: A northern California business owner printed up 3,000 color coupons and distributed them around town. He viewed it as a low-cost guerrilla marketing tactic, and his sales actually went *down*. Why? Because regular customers who normally would have paid full price took advantage of the discount. But that isn't all; it cost him *over* $900 to print those coupons. Remember—a great business makes about three cents on the dollar; he had to generate $30,000 in business *just to break even* on that promotion!

Instead of playing Santa Claus to your customers, you must focus solely on your four walls. If you can't, there may not be a market for your goods or services; that's sad, but that's capitalism. It is your responsibility to make a profit; don't blame the banks, Obama, or anyone else.

And no—there is no such thing as a level playing field. Wal-Mart will always be able to undercut your price; Starbucks will always be able to get a better location; and Best Buy will always be able to out-market you. The mall will always have better parking than a downtown shopping district. It's not whine and cry but rather change or die. The choice is yours, and the time to act is now.

You need to use a variety of arrows to hit the loyal, profitable target customer (see Figure 8.1). You must improve your customers' and employees' experiences if you want to succeed. You must display your merchandise where it's best featured, rather than wherever there happens to be space. You have to carry items that aren't readily available at the mass merchants to give your store a unique personality. Fixing your store may mean having to start all over with training your employees; it might even mean hiring a whole new crew. While that is indeed frustrating, it's necessary. I let eight employees go within a few weeks of my arrival at one store, yet I had a record-breaking month. Was it tough? Heck yes, but I'd rather have four high-energy salespeople who were committed than a dozen hangers-on dragging me down.

FIGURE 8.1 A Business with a Variety of Arrows Can Hit the Profitable Customer Target

When you use the Five Parts to a Successful Sale and adopt new processes to hire and train your sales team, you minimize things falling through the cracks. You build a sales culture that rewards the best and gets rid of those who are costing you money and failing to bring profits. You then have the ability to consistently deliver exceptional results every day.

When I came onboard to help Mike Sheldrake, he lost all but one employee within one month. His regular customers called me "El Diablo" and predicted I'd ruin the business. While that was, of course, painful to hear, I'd rather you know that this very well may happen to you. The bright side is that as you stick with it, when you hire, train, and manage better, you can increase sales by double digits. Mike's sales rose 50 percent over the previous year and 40 percent over *that* the following year, which came from enhancing his customers' experience, not wringing his hands about Starbucks.

The system I've shared with you in this book is the same one I've used to help thousands of businesses succeed and now you have access to it, too. It isn't a matter of just getting more people in the door—you have to use all the tools in this book to capture customers looking for you, give them such an outstanding shopping experience that you are the only place they'd shop, follow up with them after a sale, help them brag about you, and keep in contact with them on a regular basis.

Keep your attention focused away from how everyone else is doing; that's a recipe for disaster. It's easy to place blame for low sales on a scapegoat. "They're all on the Internet; it's a recession; they're all shopping with their iPhones; or all my customers are at (fill in the name of other retailer)." You might lose faith in your customers when you know they've seen something better—and you realize that you've been taking them for granted. The good news is you can change with the next person who calls on the phone or walks through your doors.

Once a customer makes a request or has a problem that an owner or manager doesn't take seriously, this is the moment of truth. "Sorry" just doesn't work anymore; wronged Feelers will rally against you on sites like Yelp.com, TripAdvisor.com, or their own Facebook pages. You must remain focused, be consistent, and get creative. That means letting go of what might have worked well only a couple years ago and embracing the Internet so people who are looking for your products can find you (see Figure 8.2). It means using Facebook, YouTube, and other social media sites in order to hold on to existing customers like never before and help shape the intent of their friends of where to shop. And most important, you have to sell your merch at a profit.

This book is not a silver bullet; simply reading it won't automatically change your business. At this point, you need to realize that you can be as happy and successful as you make up your mind to be. Those who prefer to complain that it's not their fault that their business is struggling probably stopped reading this book early on because it was too much work for them. Thank goodness that's not you! You

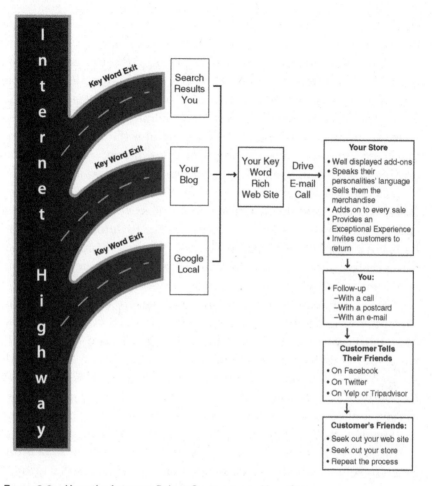

FIGURE 8.2   How the Internet Drives Customers to Your Store

now need to set goals so you have markers on your own progress. You have to be willing to do what others *won't* now, so you can do what others *can't* later, but that can be hard when you don't feel good about your business.

After I graduated high school, I got a job at a department store because I had no formal training to do anything else. I put myself through college working there and then at a job selling shoes. Other college guys looked down on me because I was working retail; they went off to do fun things while I bagged socks and asked if the customer had our credit card. There were certainly times where I felt like a loser.

While there are a few cases where people choose to go into retail, most of us back into our profession and our part-time jobs become our careers. You may not feel worthy of respect, yet according to Encyclopedia.com, there are over 19.8 million people in the United States working in retail establishments. Retail is the economic engine that keeps the economy moving. But does anyone regard retail as anything other than something to be pitied? How about you?

Like an overweight contender on NBC's hit series *The Biggest Loser,* you can treat the symptoms, but unless you uncover the root cause—your own self-image—you're likely to return to your bad habits. It's simply human nature. So take a moment and think about how you feel about working in retail. How do others see you? Would you want your child to go into retail? Why or why not?

I ask attendees in some of my retail sales training workshops, "Would you call yourself a salesperson?" It is rare to find five who would in a crowd. When I ask a follow-up, "How many of you would want your child to grow up to be a salesperson?" Even fewer hands go up. When I ask them why being a salesperson isn't desirable, they respond with the following reasons: "no security, having to kiss ass, phony, limited potential, long hours, and so on."

Retail is *selling.* Old-timers know this, but many run from it nowadays. Yet it's vital to realize that everyone is selling *something.* Begin by selling yourself on the notion that you are a person worthy of respect. You have to do that to yourself before you can sell your crew on the idea that you are an employer worth working for or sell a customer your widgets.

How to Handle Pushback from Longtime Employees

When I start working with a client, everyone is very enthused; it's the honeymoon period. The owners, managers, and employees are positive and excited during training. But when they get back to their stores, they often receive pushback from one or more employees who say, "I don't feel comfortable doing this."

They challenge their managers by asking questions like, "Why do we have to change?" You may even hear complaints from your management staff such as, "I can't get my employees to do this."

While your new employees will have no problem with the Five Parts to a Successful Sale and will be able to easily model the correct behavior, some veterans are bound to chafe. These employees hope that these new standards will be some kind of flavor of the month and pass, because your veterans are nervous you might fire them. That's why they may make snide remarks or go overboard saying exactly the same thing to show how "robotic" they sound. Their frustration and fear suddenly makes these people, who you thought were going to be able to grow your business, sabotage you much like the fifteenth-century workers who threw their shoes into the gears of the textile looms to break the cogs, fearing the machines would render them useless.

If you waver at all with the more senior employees and don't hold them to 100 percent compliance like your new employees or otherwise let your new training go, you will indeed send the message that this, too, shall pass. So here's how to handle them:

- ◆ Take your manager, assistant, or senior employee to a one-on-one coffee meeting.
- ◆ Discuss any positive outcomes, acknowledge new behaviors, or share any growth in sales you've seen since implementing the changes.
- ◆ Set forth the expectation that you need employees to support your new system 100 percent.
- ◆ Ask them what's not working for them or whether anything is frustrating them. Your goal is to lance the boil; you don't want to have to have this conversation again.
- ◆ Ask after each point, "Is there anything else?" Continue until they say something like, "No, I think that's it." Then ask, "Can you support this 100 percent?" And when they

(continued)

(*continued*)

> answer, "Yes," finish the conversation by saying, "Good;
> I'm glad I can count on you. Because I never want to have
> this conversation again."
>
> ◆ Don't offer to change or modify any of your new training;
>   your resolve is being tested.
> ◆ Tell them that if you hear anything but 100 percent
>   support of the program after that meeting, their jobs
>   will be at stake.

When you started this book, you were unaware of what you weren't doing for your business, almost like that old saying, "ignorance is bliss." As you progressed through each chapter, you became increasingly conscious of everything that you didn't know. Several things that you might have considered normal were challenged, which can feel scary. Even though my goal is to help, not hurt, depending on your personality type; you may have pulled back at some of the frank recommendations. As you begin to implement and try these various new ideas, you may fail at first. That's okay; just stick with it. At this stage of the learning curve, you're becoming more mindful of what you don't know and are taking baby steps in your quest to improve your business. Our ultimate goal is mastery—a scenario in which you can easily use Windows of Contact in a conversation and not have to remind yourself to notice something about her, or look forward to reviewing your crews' average number of items report each Monday without having to put a reminder in your Outlook calendar.

Starting out in business can be likened to a wedding; you think the sky is the limit. You rent the space regardless of common-area maintenance charges; you buy what is cute and adorable; you hire friends. But after you've been in retail a while, you may feel dragged down by the ball and chain of the business. This is especially true if you've essentially bought a job and not the freedom-enhancing moneymaker you thought your store might be. You may even be thinking of leaving, so you spend more time at the bank, you take more trips, you stop looking at ways to market, and you blindly trust your great staff.

Then one day you go to work and find your customers are gone with no forwarding note. They didn't tell you they wanted you to work on your business; they just stopped visiting. At that point you have to pull the carrot of your business out of the ground and look at the roots. Much like a marriage where two people have grown apart, you are smack dab in the middle of a crisis. Do you work on it or walk away? The choice is yours, but you have to realize that it was your choices—not someone else's—that got you here in the first place.

The big changes—repainting, remerchandising, hiring some new team members—are easy to make, but you always have to be on guard against reverting to your old ways. It's like a dieter who switches from his whole milk latte to drip coffee to lose weight, and, after a while, tries a two-percent milk latte. He sees no dire effects, so it's pretty easy (and pretty tasty) to try the whole milk latte once again. Not too long after that, he'll begin to complain that he can never lose weight and start wearing that as some kind of armor that says, "I've tried dozens of diets, but none work." The slippery slope starts with lowering expectations, so you need to inspect what you expect.

Lifetime Value of a Customer

When I worked in the coffeehouse business, we discovered the stunning lifetime value of a customer that showed the true value of a missed opportunity if a new customer doesn't come back. An average customer order was $4. A regular came into the shop once a day five days a week, which equaled around $1,000 a year. Local demographics indicated that people moved about once every four to five years. Those details let us realize that grabbing a new customer and providing an exceptional experience, if we did it right, was worth about $4,500. Likewise, if we did it wrong it wasn't $4 we were losing but $4,500. Figuring out the lifetime value of a customer can help you stay on track to get out from behind the castle of your counter to establish a connection with the person who just walked in.

If you let people choose between what they *want* to do and what they *have* to do, they'll do what they *want* to do. When I was working with GiftandHomechannel.com, people there told me the number one reason gift store owners went to their site was to search for new ways to display merchandise. Of course that's what they *want* to do; they don't want to worry about open-to-buy levels or their financials. It's like saying, "If I know how to display an item or frame a picture, well then, I'll be fine." But that's a false sense of control. They don't want to admit they are chronic overbuyers, because that would mean they couldn't spend all their money at the merchandise marts. It would, however, let them see that their money was sitting on the sales floor, and no amount of clever display techniques could solve that until they admitted they didn't pay attention to their open- to-buy. Unless you have a spouse making boatloads of money that allows you to avoid fiscal responsibility, you can't continue that way.

Do you want to fix your business and return it to its former glory? Sell it? Or grow it to new heights? Those are your three choices. Getting a business healthy is simple, but it is not easy. As it does with any plan to change, the old saying "nothing good is ever accomplished without hard work" applies here as well. If you want to sell it, realize that no one will buy a business that does not make a profit. So you may have to force yourself to make the choices necessary to grow it. You'll have to hit it with everything you've got, because you could lose everything including the store, your credit, and your house.

The changes you must implement might make you feel like you're on a diet in some cases. For instance, you must have the discipline to buy only in response to inventory changes. Another might feel like training for a marathon, while others may feel like they're going to school to learn to deal with the financials. Sometimes, you will feel like a psychologist attempting to type the four personalities or learning a new language to speak to them. You'll be finding the best parts of yourself as you make each of these different discoveries. You can bite off a bit each week with this book as your guide—and make a huge difference in profitability. You may also be interested in the companion home study course detailed at the back of the book.

How Your Personality Type Can Grow Your Business

Drivers should use their natural planning abilities to create a blueprint for change and make sure to build in rewards for themselves when goals are met. While all four personalities benefit from this approach, Drivers, in particular, respond well to specific and measurable goals. Give yourself daily, weekly, and monthly activities and standards to which you hold yourself personally accountable (see Chapter 1). You must feel all of the work is worth it, or you will be doomed to failure. Change is the very thing that stokes your ego, so get on your horse and save the day. Try not to be too impatient and cut your nose off to spite your face; only fire an employee when you have someone else on board to replace him.

While it is clear you are the chief, you will need others to make this work, so polish your team-building skills. Go out after work sometime with your staff or throw a bowling party—anything that breaks the pattern of work, work, work. Slow down, explain yourself, and carefully listen to others' concerns as you adopt your new skills. You don't have to agree with any of them, but you don't want to shut down your Feelers; they just want to know you are listening to them. A good way to convey this is to summarize what you heard them say and ask if you got it right. All most people really want is to know that you heard them.

Analyticals should first write down and prioritize their list of things to do, putting the hardest first: improving their people and selling skills. You already have the charts and graphs of sales; now comes the fun of using your natural ability to track progress. Stop hiding in the back office and engage your crew! If you've hired people just like you, they will resist any change because it's hard for them. Come up with logical reasons why executing this program can prevent all or most of the symptoms you've been experiencing. Then train them so there is no chance for embarrassment on the sales floor. Quiet the voice that's asking "what if?" and choose instead to use your natural ability to strategize and problem solve. While you naturally tend to measure people on their preciseness and results, you'll need to shift your priority from having them stocking shelves to selling merch.

Hire an Expressive personality to inject some energy into your crew and pick up your own pace.

If you are an Expressive yourself, make a list of all the things you'd like to do, then match the items to the chapters in this book. You learn by doing, so get out there and try things. Your natural flexibility allows you to adapt to new things, but your relaxed attitude can make you think you have plenty of time to get this done; don't let it. Use your inherent ability to multitask and allow your keen eye for opportunity to shine as you once again bring the excitement you have for life into your business. You can get irritated with routine but that's exactly what you need—especially when it comes to training staff. Do the work; don't talk too much about it. Don't get more books to read and programs to try; stick with this one and do the hard work. While your spontaneous nature can make work fun, a methodical approach will keep you on track. You'll want to hire others with personalities unlike your own to break the "clubby" feel of your store, and you'll need to curb the sarcasm of those around you. You're not known as a stickler for details like an Analytical, so write down exactly what you are going to do and by when. Hang up the phone and be truly present with your crew and customers when you are in your store. Stay focused on all the opportunities you are creating—and realize that change takes time.

Amiables, know that your preference for maintaining the status quo will make this transition difficult for you. You'll need to embrace change because it's good for you, don't fear it. Close relationships are important, but they shouldn't be with your employees or it will limit your effectiveness in managing them. Consider getting someone you know (that you do *not* work with) to act as a running buddy, someone to share your joys and challenges and not someone who'll be satisfied listening to sob stories. You naturally measure people's worth by how well they get along with others but that is not the quality needed to move sales. You'll probably need to develop a tougher skin when dealing with employees so you don't take everything personally. With their natural high energy level, hire a Driver or an Expressive to challenge you and you'll find work much more fun. While your natural inclination is to be nice and to *listen,* you'll now need to *tell* people what to do—and hold them accountable for their actions. Any problems you encounter are just business; remember, you are not your feelings, so deal with any conflict directly and don't wait. Employees will naturally test you more than they would other personalities, so use write-ups to your advantage. If results do not improve by the given deadline, then let these people go. Squash your need to be liked and your fear of conflict. Use your natural ability to forgive yourself for any shortcomings. Realize that today is a new day, and use your innate people skills to reinvent your crew.

No matter what your dominant personality type is, make what you've learned in these pages a blueprint for making your business successful. See if you can identify what needs to be improved, and do those five things at the end of each chapter. If you do, you'll be more than halfway there.

You can join my Facebook fan page and keep the dialogue about your progress going with me and other readers. You may want to join my mentor program to get weekly coaching or opt to use some of the additional resources available to augment this book; these include spreadsheets, mystery shops, or a phone consult with me. Whatever you choose, remember that you *can* make your business work.

If you want to grow even more, call me. The Retail Doctor® does make house calls. Whatever you do, don't do a story in the local paper about how you can't compete—*because you can.*

Good selling!
—Bob

The 13 Steps to Being a Top Salesperson

1. Maintain a positive attitude toward yourself and your work. When something goes wrong, don't waste time complaining; work toward its correction.

2. Understand that a clean and organized store directly correlates to high sales.

3. Approach more customers with the goal of selling something, not merely clerking.

4. Realize that customers are on the defensive. Make a personal remark that demands a positive answer and puts the customer at ease. Share something you have in common based on the customer's answer.

5. Never say, "Can I help you?" "How are you?" or "Anything else?"

6. Carry a prop when approaching a customer and move away quickly to let the customer browse. Return within a few minutes and continue to build rapport.

7. Ask questions that open windows; try not to ask anything that can be answered with a "No."

8. Know the store's stock and don't oversell limited items.

9. Never come out of the stockroom empty-handed. If something is sold out, present something similar.

10. Offer additional products and accessories at the close of the sale.

11. Locate out-of-stock items from other stores, or suggest that you special order other alternatives for customers. Take a deposit to ensure that the customer really wants the item.

12. Understand the merchandise: its price points, construction, wear, and how it compares to other brands and competitors. Ask about new products before a customer does.

13. Come around the counter and thank customers by name at the time of sale and again with a short note the following day.

Examples of Forms and Updates

Throughout the book, you've been referred to examples of forms in the back of the book. In an effort to keep them current, these have been included on a separate update page for the book.

These forms include:

- Manager Job Description
- Employee Review
- Employee Warning
- Training Badge Example
- Mystery Shop Resource

All of these forms are available online at www.retaildoc.com/guide/update.php.

While you're there you'll find updates to the book, as well as bonus material.

About the Author

Bob Phibbs is the Retail Doctor®, an internationally recognized expert on business strategy, customer service, sales, and marketing. With over 30 years' experience beginning in the trenches of retail and extending to senior management positions, he has been a corporate officer, franchisor, and entrepreneur. Phibbs is a popular speaker because he knows what business owners are up against, since he has started three successful businesses and can deliver the message to "look in the mirror," with a straightforward, witty, and detailed process to grow sales.

Phibbs has creatively helped some of retail's best-known brands and their dealers, including Yamaha, Caswell-Massey, Hunter Douglas, LEGO, and Brother succeed. He is a frequent guest on MSNBC's *Your Business*. His Advanced Sales Training weekends using his Five Parts to a Successful Sale have boosted stores' sales by over 20 percent within months.

After completing his degree at Chapman University and attending USC, Bob fulfilled an as-yet-untapped dream of wearing cowboy clothes every day while selling high-end boots and hats to the city slickers of Los Angeles County during the height of the Urban Cowboy trend. Bob's part-time job soon became a career, and he built a network of over 55 stores at the top of their industry.

In 1994, Bob started his own consulting company, The Retail Doctor®, with a mission to provide training, inspiration, and hope to independent businesses; to teach them how to successfully compete in today's retail environment. By helping a coffee roaster that had been in business 25 years reverse a protracted sales drop-off, compete against a second Starbucks just 75 feet from his front door, and increase sales by 50 percent in one year, Bob found a national audience.

In 1998, the *Los Angeles Times* courted Bob to perform business makeovers. He began speaking about his success principles, which grew to include manufacturers and trade associations around the world.

Bob provided sales training for the elite Hunter Douglas Gallery alliance program, creating a culture of selling excellence to support a strong national distribution of over 400 dealers. Bob put his successive strategies for improving a business into his first book, *You Can Compete: Double Sales Without Discounting.*

Bob drank up the next big trend helping It's A Grind Coffee, a startup, first as COO and then as VP of Marketing. Along the way, they grew to over 125 franchised locations nationwide, and created a lot of buzz as the featured coffeehouse on Showtime's *Weeds.* Phibbs helped make It's A Grind the second-fastest growing company in Los Angeles County two years running, according to the *Los Angeles Business Journal.*

Phibbs programs and his work have been featured on PBS's *Life & Times, Entrepreneur* magazine, the *New York Times,* and the *Wall Street Journal.* He received the Greatest Increase in Sales Award for his work with a specialty-clothing retailer at South Coast Plaza in Southern California, the highest per-square-foot grossing mall in the world.

He recently moved to upstate New York from Los Angeles. Bob owns his own publishing firm, is a member of the Author's Guild, the National Retail Federation, and National Speakers Association; his web site is www.retaildoc.com.

Index

Firing employees, 147, 173–175
Five Guys Burgers, 158
Five Parts to a Successful Sale,
    77–116. *See also individual
    parts*
  analyzing failure of, 108–109
  and clerking vs. selling, 81–84
  closing the sale in, 102–105
  closing with an add-on in, 79,
    105–108
  features and benefits statements
    in, 78, 101–102
  greeting in, 77–78, 84–92,
    109–112
  growing your business with,
    213–214
  and personality type, 79–81
  pushback against, 109–112,
    216–218
  question to help narrow choices
    in, 78, 99–100
  training in, *see* Training
  Windows of Contact in, 78,
    92–99
  and worst questions to ask,
    113–114
Flags, 45
Fleming, Linda Abrams, 104–105
Flip camera, 197
Floor banners, 45
Floor design, 26–27
Focus:
  narrowing, 4–6
  for profitability, 18
Followers (Twitter), 199
Forms, 227
Friends of employees, hiring, 65
Fun, xiii. *See also* Expressives

G
Gage, Randy, xvi
The Gap, 26

Gardner, Meghan, 112–113
GiftandHomechannel.com,
    220
Glen, Peter, 36
Goals:
  for cashier upselling, 108
  employee, 153–154
  for greeting customers, 110
  rewards for meeting, 221
  setting, 153
  Shark Charts of, 156–157
Goal sheets, 153–156
Go Daddy, 179
Google:
  adwords, 181
  checking applicant information
    on, 75
  Local Business Center, 186–188
  pay-per-click ads on, 203–204
  search accuracy of, 180
  and title bar keywords, 181
  YouTube and key word searches,
    197
Grand Openings, 206
Greeting customers, 77–78, 84–92,
    109–112
  attitude in, 85–87
  goals for, 110
  and Hell Zone, 88
  props for, 89–90
  pushback from employees about,
    109–112
  and store tours, 90
  timing of, 84–85
  training for, 125
  words used in, 84
Grids of store, 23–24
Groups:
  Facebook, 193
  Twitter, 199
Grouping items, for displays,
    40

Could You Use Some Extra Help?
This Doctor Makes House Calls!

Get even more out of this book with the Home Study Course

Sometimes staying motivated and organized is complicated. Guarantee your success by staying connected to Bob Phibbs to ensure you lose your bad habits that are keeping you from being profitable. Having this kind of support can be the difference between reaching the finish line and running in place.

With this Home Study Course, you'll first be taken on a detailed exploration of your business that will give you a report card that you can use to really affect change in your business. The second part shows you what the information in the report card means. The final section gives you ways to change those areas that aren't directly making you money

Included in the Home Study Course are two Mystery shops from the nation's leader in objective reporting of a customer's experience in your store.

Even better, once you get the report card results, you are entitled to a free session talking directly with Bob to help you strategize how you can increase sales in tune with your own personality.

Sound good?

It is and here's one of the best parts—you can do this all at your own pace.

Your downloadable Home Study Course ordering details are available at www.retaildoc.com/makeover.html.

Not sure you can do it by yourself? Couple it with the Mentor program and you get one-on-one weekly mentoring, with Bob personally helping you achieve your goals.

Like Reading the Book?

How about taking it to the next level?

Speaking Engagements

"If you want to witness something amazing and totally different, you ought to catch Bob Phibbs! My customers could not get enough of this energetic seminar filled with tons of exercises that truly got you thinking about your business, while also keeping the passion. Typically in an industry such as ours (picture framing glass), it was assumed that there was not much more you could do to get your customers excited about glass. But with Bob's tips on thinking outside of the box and his Five Steps to a Successful Sale, there has been a paradigm shift. If I hadn't been there to witness it myself, I wouldn't believe it. Do yourself and your customers a favor and present one of Bob's seminars; believe me, it will be a business-changing experience." — Anissa Burrell-Butler

Phibbs addresses thousands of retailers internationally in keynote addresses, talks, seminars, and presentations up to three days in length. Wouldn't you like a positive message that conveys the perfect blend of street-smart success strategies with humor and fun?

His topics include:
- *Your Team's Personality Styles May Be Killing Your Business*
- *How The Four Personality Types To Grow Your Business*
- *You Can Compete: Double Sales Without Discounting*
- *Presentation Is Everything*

Audiences are sky high during his trainings because he understands their needs and presents his information with both wit and passion. To have him appear at your next event, e-mail Bob@retaildoc.com or call 518-444-8082.

Mentor Program

Bob also offers one-on-one mentoring designed to make certain you succeed in all areas of your business. The objective is simple: increase your income, increase your time off, and increase your speed to profitability.

For full details on the Mentor program, visit
http://www.retaildoc.com/mentor.html